WHERE PASSION LIVES

WHERE PASSION LIVES

The Spirit of College Football

BY

DEAN C. HAWTHORNE

CFB SPIRIT PUBLISHING
LOS ANGELES
2021

This is a work of fiction. Any semblance between original characters and real persons, living or dead, is coincidental. The likenesses of historical/famous figures have been used fictitiously; the author does not speak for or represent these people. All opinions expressed in this book are the author's, or fictional.

FIRST EDITION

Cover and interior design by Barbara Aronica-Buck
Cover art created with iStock images by Peter Vahlersvik and Dmytro Aksono
Copyedited by Sue Rasmussen
Proofread by Kate Petrella

ISBN 978-1-7364811-0-3

CFB Spirit Publishing
Los Angeles

This book is dedicated to my wonderful family: Katherine, Lauren, Mason, Erika, John, Susan, Eugene, Julia, Peter, Stephanie, Lucas, Andy, Virginia, Matthew, Ryan, Lori, Keith, Seth, Hayden, Bev, Al, Wes, Darlene, Margaret, John, Gwenn, Jim, the brothers of Kappa Sigma / Delta Eta, and college football fans everywhere!

ACKNOWLEDGMENT

For any significant endeavor in life, there are few things more valuable than the help of a great coach. I want to thank Lou Aronica at The Fiction Studio for his thoughtful analysis and insightful advice throughout the writing of *Where Passion Lives*. I will always be tremendously grateful.

AUTHOR'S NOTE

Despite being a descendant of one of America's great authors, Nathaniel Hawthorne, I didn't intend to pursue a career in writing. Instead, I decided to pay the bills with a forty-year career in sales and management, while earning the opportunity to work for a few of our country's top corporations. However, writing was always a very significant part of my life and, whether it was for business or pleasure, my efforts were generally met with positive reviews. Deep down, I always held out hope that I had inherited at least a shred of my ancestor's immense talent.

But as much as I enjoy writing, it pales in comparison to my love of sports. Outside of my wonderful wife and family, there is nothing I love more. Sports have consumed most of my free time ever since I was a young boy, and if you name the game, the odds are pretty good I've either played, coached, or at least watched it over the course of my lifetime.

Topping my list of favorites is college football. No other sport rivals the thrill, passion, and traditions of America's greatest game. I've watched it as a fan and studied it as a hobby for over fifty-five years. From an early age, I was predetermined to attend USC, and the true love of my future alma mater and its powerhouse football program gripped me from the very beginning.

Several years ago, an idea for this book came to mind and it never went away. As time passed, the idea continued to grow until I became absolutely convinced that I had to write this book because if I didn't, I would forever look back with tremendous regret. Writing a novel requires a significant commitment, and it's a good strategy to choose a subject you deeply care about and have an in-depth knowledge of. For me, college football checks both those boxes.

Now that this book has found its way into your hands, my sincere hope is that it brings you as much enjoyment reading it as I experienced writing it.

Dean C. Hawthorne

CONTENTS

1

Labor Day Weekend

Labor Day weekend is one of the best times of the year. Yes, it marks the unofficial end of summer, but this weekend begins the start of one of the most exciting times of the year—the college football season. I've waited nearly eight months since early January for this weekend to roll around and it's finally here. I am a college football fanatic.

The anticipation for the upcoming season has been building for the past month with all the hype the media can muster. Fall training camp is over, the preseason polls have been released, and people across the country anxiously await the kickoff.

Since the end of last season, I occupied myself with the NBA and college basketball, Major League Baseball, and the NFL. Along the way, I've followed the college football recruiting wars and kept track of all the reports from spring practice and fall training camp, but now, finally, the new season is about to start.

Football is, by far, the most popular sport in the country and the National Football League is the king of the hill but, for me, college football beats everything hands down. Pro football is great, but I live in Los Angeles and the NFL left us high and dry for over twenty years when both the Rams and Raiders packed up and left town. The teams blamed Los Angeles for a lack of support from the fans and the city, which prevented them from being competitive. But if you put an inferior product on the field, don't be surprised when the fans don't show up.

I grew up without the NFL and it was difficult to develop an allegiance toward any of the other teams across the country. I don't bet on games or play fantasy football, but I did keep an eye on the league once the playoffs rolled around because everything's sudden death and there are always some great games. It just doesn't hold much interest for me when you don't really care who wins. Living in Los Angeles, I'm not going to spend my time indoors watching teams from Green Bay or Seattle when we've got great weather year-round and the beaches, mountains and deserts right in our backyard. I'd rather enjoy the outdoors than sit on the couch expanding my waistline.

Now that the Rams have returned to LA, along with the Chargers, pro football is back in a big way. I love the game and couldn't help getting caught up in the Rams' run to the Super Bowl a few years ago. If the Rams and Chargers prove that they have a commitment to winning and show it on the field, they'll do fine here. LA's a big place and there are more than enough people to support two pro teams.

The one thing I will give everything else up for, no matter when or where, is watching my alma mater play. I'm a USC alumnus and work for the school's athletic department. Football is a huge part of being a Trojan and USC has one of the great college football traditions in the country. Whenever they play, I am either at the game or else watching on TV.

This long holiday weekend, USC and other schools from across the country kick off their seasons and I am getting away for a well-deserved break. The Trojans are opening their season on the road so I'm going to catch the game on TV. A friend of mine has a vacation home up in the mountains and has offered to let me use it for the weekend. He calls it a cabin but it's really a large, secluded home on several acres with an incredible view. More important, it's got all the amenities including a giant flat screen and satellite, so I won't miss any of the action. I'll be spending the next three days hiking, fishing, relaxing and watching a lot of football.

My name is Kyle. I'm a twenty-eight-year-old Director of Development at USC. Development is a fancy name for fundraising and work has been extremely demanding recently. The job requires long hours including nights and weekends and I've got to get away for some down time on my own to recharge my batteries. I was able to clear my schedule to get the holiday weekend off and I'm really looking forward to the brief vacation. Getting out of town late Friday evening; the traffic has died down and the freeways are clear. It's a beautiful night.

Along the way, I pass a Marine Corps recruiting billboard. The image reminds me of my dad in his dress blues standing with Mom in their wedding photo shortly after he returned home from the Gulf War. He died when I was twelve years old, and my memories of him include some of the most wonderful times of my life but also some of the most painful. Dad spent much of his free time with me and nearly all of it involved sports. No matter what we were doing he always found a way to make things fun. I loved hearing his inspirational stories of the middleweight titles he won on the Marine Corps boxing team. I idolized him, perhaps to the exclusion of realizing he was human like everyone else. He carried some deep emotional scars from the war that never healed. At night he drank heavily, saying he needed it to help him sleep, but he couldn't hide his suffering. It was agonizing to watch it slowly destroy him. He gave so much of himself to me but when he died, I was just left with heartbreak and anger.

As I start to get off the highway and make the climb into the mountains, I look forward to leaving the LA heat and smog behind and breathing some fresh mountain air. I roll down the windows, turn up the music and try to leave the stress of the city in my rearview mirror.

• • •

The drive passes quickly and I'm at the cabin before I know it. Pulling into the entrance, I follow the winding driveway up to the house. One of the perks of working in development is the opportunity to develop relationships with wealthy alumni and donors who are committed to supporting the success of the athletic department. John Moore, the fellow that owns this house, is a brilliant businessman and alumnus who lives and dies with the football program. He and I became friends over the last few years, and he has been very generous in letting me use his place from time to time. Usually, I'll bring a couple of buddies along but this time I wanted to be on my own and just unwind. The solitude up here can be very re-energizing.

I turn on the lights and fire up the TV to make sure the satellite is working and set the DVR to record ESPN's College GameDay first thing in the morning. Here on the West Coast it starts quite early on Saturday morning. I always record it back home and check it out after I wake up and get my workout in. It's late, so I head for bed to get an early start in the morning.

• • •

The alarm goes off and as I'm waking up all I hear is silence—wonderful peace and quiet—which is a rarity back home in the city surrounded by neighbors and traffic, but up here it's a way of life. I pull back the shades and look out at an awesome day surrounded by tall pines, bright sunshine and an amazing view of the mountains. There isn't another cabin anywhere in sight.

I fill up on a big breakfast and load my backpack with some snacks and water for the morning hike. It's a terrific trail about ten miles long with a big climb up and over a massive granite peak. The view from the top is well worth the effort.

• • •

When I return to the cabin, I play back College GameDay to check out their rundown of the day's games from around the country. My excitement at the start of each new season is always tempered by my disappointment of not being able to live out my dreams of playing college football. My father began training me from birth to be an elite athlete and he coached me in every sport I played. His vision of seeing me play football for USC and going on to the NFL became my driving ambition. I wanted it more than anything and it was the only thing I've ever had a true passion for in my life.

By the time I finished high school I was on track to take the next step in college. I was the highest-rated running back in California and one of the top recruited players in the country. SC offered me a scholarship and, by the end of fall training camp, I earned the opportunity to start at tailback as a true freshman. In the week leading up to our first game my heart gave out during practice. After months of recovery, the doctors told me I would never be able to play again. I've been a spectator ever since.

• • •

Finally, a few hours later it's time for the SC game to kick off. The Trojans are in Knoxville to start the season against the University of Tennessee. The Vols are a tradition-rich program from the ultra-competitive SEC. The game is one of the top matchups of the day as the preseason polls have both schools ranked in the top ten and the game is nationally televised. A Tennessee home game at Neyland Stadium is instantly recognizable on TV because of the unmistakable orange and white checkerboard end zones. The Volunteers' marching band plays "Rocky Top," the school's unofficial fight song, and the crowd sings along as they get ready for kickoff. My pregame nerves make it impossible to sit down and relax. I'm over two thousand miles away in the comfort of a beautiful home in the mountains with a spectacular view, but my anxiety level is so high it's almost as if I was on the field getting ready to play.

SC wins the coin toss and elects to receive. The teams line up for the kickoff and Tennessee's boot goes out of bounds and we get excellent field position at the thirty-five-yard line to start the game. We're breaking in a new quarterback and over one hundred thousand screaming Vols fans are on their feet making it tough for the players to hear. SC breaks the huddle but there's confusion at the line of scrimmage waiting for the snap. Vance Richards, the quarterback, looks shaky and has to call timeout just before the play clock expires. He jogs to the sideline and you can see the frustration on the coaches' faces trying to get the kid to calm down. The crowd has made an immediate impact by disrupting USC which fuels their enthusiasm, and they're even louder as we line up again out of the timeout. We manage to get the snap off and Richards drops back to pass. He has time and takes a shot down the middle of the field, but the ball sails several yards over the receiver's head. We try to run on the next play, but it's stuffed a yard deep in our backfield. Third and eleven, we try a wheel route to the tailback but Richards leads him too far upfield and the ball is nearly intercepted by a linebacker who read the play perfectly and had nothing but open grass ahead of him. Man, did we dodge a bullet there. Not a great start, especially on the road when you want to have some early success and try to take the crowd out of the game. Our punter lines up to kick it away and almost misses the ball. He shanks it off his foot and the ball sails wide left out of bounds barely crossing mid-field. I press pause on the remote and restrain myself from putting my foot through the TV screen. I go out on the back deck to get some air. "What is going on?" I ask myself. We should be better prepared than this. We definitely don't look like a top ten team right now.

Tennessee smells blood and immediately drives down the field for an easy score. Our offense sputters again and we have to give the ball right back. The Vols look well coached and put together a long, clock-eating drive for a touchdown right at the end of the first quarter. Tennessee has got SC back on its heels and has punched us right in the mouth: Tennessee 14, USC 0.

We get the ball to start the second quarter and our offense begins to find some momentum. We commit to running the ball as opposed to panicking and trying to get it all back at once. Our success on the ground takes some pressure off Richards and he starts to find a rhythm with his receivers. We score ten unanswered points in the quarter to claw our way back and give our defense a little break.

• • •

In the second half, the game plays out as expected between two tough opponents. We're deep into the fourth quarter with the score tied seventeen all and a little more than six minutes to play. It's crunch time and the tension of the game continues to build. I just made a chili dog to help satisfy my nervous cravings.

We have the ball and are driving at the Tennessee forty-five-yard line. Richards drops back to pass, good protection, plenty of time. He's looking right, then looks left and sees a wide-open receiver streaking down the sideline. He reaches back and delivers a perfect spiral that will give the Trojans the go-ahead score. I'm on my feet yelling at the top of my lungs and just as I take a big bite of chili dog, a Tennessee defender comes out of nowhere to intercept the pass at the five-yard line. I gasp in disbelief and suck a big chunk of hot dog down my windpipe. I immediately try to cough it up, but nothing happens. I can't cough, I can't speak, and I can't breathe. That hot dog is stuck and I'm choking!

It's scary when you're not able to breathe, even more so when there's no one around to help. I've got to stay calm and recall the emergency training I've had. I make a fist with one hand and put it over my stomach below my rib cage. I grab my fist with the other hand and begin thrusting it inward to try and dislodge the obstruction. It's not coming loose. I go to the kitchen and bend over the back of a chair and start ramming my midsection down on it as hard as I can. The force of the thrusts is cracking my ribs but nothing's working. I run to the phone and dial 9-1-1. With no way to speak, I know they'll at least be able to identify the address from the call and send out help. When the operator answers I tap out a Morse code SOS on the dial pad. She picks up on the distress signal and asks me to confirm. I tap out another signal and she says help is on the way.

There's no more time. I recall a video I saw about paramedics who perform an emergency tracheotomy to save a choking victim, so I grab a steak knife from the counter to cut an opening in my windpipe. I bend over to look at my reflection in the toaster and locate the notch just below my Adam's apple. As I put the knife to my throat and start to cut, everything goes dark.

My upper body collapses on the counter and the knife jams into my throat, severing my carotid artery. Blood is gushing from my neck as I crumple to the floor.

Lying in a widening pool of blood, I feel a strange but peaceful sense that my body is slowly shutting down. I can faintly hear the TV in the other room as the announcer says, "Tennessee has scored the go-ahead touchdown on a sensational ninety-five-yard interception return and now leads USC twenty-four to seventeen. We'll be right back after these commercial messages." I wish I could say the same thing.

They say hot dogs aren't very good for you. I would have to agree.

2

Now What?

An infinite void of darkness and tranquility surrounds me. I'm conscious but see nothing, hear nothing and feel nothing. I just am.

Slowly the obscurity begins to give way to light. As if I'm waking from a deep sleep, a strange sensation is lifting me upward. I continue to rise and see that I am pulling away from my body lying on the floor. It's a bloody mess. The steak knife is still stuck in my throat.

I drift around the room and pass by a mirror hanging on the wall. Looking in the glass and not seeing your reflection staring back is an eerie feeling. I'm here—I just don't show up in the mirror, not even a trace. Now I know how Dracula must feel.

The telephone remains connected to 9-1-1 and I can hear chatter from the operator on the other end. I imagine she'll probably stay on the line until the police arrive.

Isn't there supposed to be some sort of light or portal that draws you into the afterlife? Maybe the Grim Reaper is coming by but he's running a little late. This is terribly anticlimactic; I was expecting something a little more dramatic. The game is still going on TV and Tennessee continues to lead by seven with just under two minutes to play. USC has the ball and is driving downfield. At least I can watch the end of the game, but just as I settle onto the couch, a loud banging jolts me back to reality.

"Police, open the door!"

The knocking at the front door continues while a patrolman comes around to the back of the house and cautiously enters through the sliding glass door. With his gun drawn, he walks through the living room, passing right by me. The house is quiet except for the sound of the game on TV. He moves to the front door and lets his partner in.

"What have you got?"

"Don't know."

They pass by the telephone receiver and hear the voice of the 9-1-1 operator still on the line.

One of them picks up the phone. "Hello, this is Deputy Edwards. We just arrived but there doesn't seem to be anyone here. We haven't searched the house yet. What did you hear on the call?"

She explains that no one ever spoke on the line. "Whoever called tapped out an SOS a couple of times and a few minutes later, I heard a thud," she says, "so we put the dispatch out to send you guys over. Didn't hear anything else until you guys arrived."

"Okay thanks, we'll take it from here," responded the officer.

They approach the kitchen and see my body lying on the floor.

"Uh, oh. What happened here?" The officer kneels down to

check for a pulse as if knowing there's no chance. "He's gone. Call this in and get homicide and forensics up here. I'll check the rest of the house."

The police aren't sure what happened. It could be a murder, maybe suicide. After going through the rest of the house, one of the officers is attracted to the game on TV and starts to watch. His partner returns from the patrol car.

"Hey Carl, SC's on TV, looks like a great game. They're down by seven to Tennessee; not much time left."

They both grab seats in front of the TV and I join them to watch the end of the game.

• • •

USC wins in a triple overtime thriller and the patrolmen jump up from their seats when a few plainclothes policemen walk in. The officers give the detectives a download on what they know, and I've got a front row seat to the investigation.

They're taking pictures of everything. One of them says, "No forced entry, no apparent signs of a struggle." The forensics guy rolls my body over and quickly identifies signs of asphyxiation. Rather than a murderous stab to the neck, he speculates the knife wound was a failed attempt at a desperate, do-it-yourself tracheotomy. Having noticed the half-eaten chili dog in the living room when he arrived, he says, "I'm guessing he was choking and tried to cut open his trachea." He straddles my lifeless body and gives a forceful thrust to the upper abdomen. The deadly piece of tube steak comes flying out of my mouth like a cork shot out of a champagne bottle. "There's our killer," he says.

They find my wallet and identification and do a records search, which tells them I'm not the owner of the property. They'll have to notify my friend John to let him know what happened and determine if I was there with his permission or trespassing. The forensics man collects the steak knife, the chunk of hot dog, blood samples and other items in case they need to do further lab analysis, but the consensus among everyone is that it was an accidental death. The coroner zips up the body bag and carts my remains away. The police seal up the house.

• • •

Alone again, the quiet isolation I sought to find this weekend has unexpectedly become a dreaded actuality. "Where do I go from here?" I wonder.

I start thinking about my mom and the pain she'll suffer when the police contact her. She's all alone now. I wish I could be there for her but if I saw her it would only tear me apart. Fortunately, I have no wife and kids; that would be even more traumatic for everyone.

I start pacing around the house. The kitchen is a disturbing sight with blood smeared over the countertop, down the cabinet and pooled on the floor. The TV is off in the living room and what remained of my chili dog is gone, taken by the lab guy along with some of my other personal belongings. My car's still in the driveway, but I won't be needing that anymore.

At least it was a great game; I literally died in the excitement. If only I could operate the TV, I'd be able to catch up on the other games. No sooner than having the thought, the screen pops on and I'm watching highlights from across the country. "Wow, that's cool. How did that happen?" As I wonder what other games are on, the screen immediately jumps to Oklahoma playing Wisconsin. Any others? With a wave of the hand, boom! Michigan is locked into a close battle with Utah. Next, Louisiana-Monroe is getting a nice payday by agreeing to suffer a beatdown at the hands of Georgia. The score is 45–0 at the half.

This is great! It seems like all I need to do to make something happen is think it into existence. I want a bigger screen, so the picture moves off the TV and becomes a giant, high-definition hologram floating in the air. I think about changing channels, wave my hand and another game comes on. I want a channel guide and it instantly shows a list of every game currently being played across the country. The hardest decision is which game to watch. I want to see multiple games at the same time, so the giant screen divides and shows me eight games at once. I can control the camera angles of each game and get a complete, unrestricted view from anywhere inside the stadium. I get comfortable on the couch and watch game after game, finishing with Boise State playing at Hawaii, which wraps up around one o'clock in the morning. I may be dead, and I don't think this is heaven, but so far, it's not bad.

I'm not tired so I bring up a list of movies that shows every film ever made. It's Netflix on steroids. I scroll through the lineup and *Heaven Can Wait* seems like an appropriate choice. It's the 1978 version of the film where Warren Beatty plays a reincarnated quarterback for the Los Angeles Rams. After finishing that, I watch a couple more movies until dawn breaks and finally, I've had enough.

As a spirit, I don't seem to need sleep or food or anything else for that matter. I have been freed from the bonds of human existence so it's time to explore my ghostly abilities. Doors, walls and other solid objects shouldn't present any obstacles for me. I press my hand against the front door and it goes right through as if it's a mirage. I continue outside and feel the warmth of the sun and smell the fresh mountain air. It's a beautiful morning, the kind that makes you glad to be alive. I wish I were.

I've always had dreams about being able to fly and now I can soar just like Superman. Sailing hundreds of feet in the air, I glide above the hills and treetops. I circle back over the house and dive like a missile straight toward the roof, piercing it like a hot knife through butter and stopping on a dime right back in the living room. The feeling of complete freedom takes over my thoughts. I can go anywhere I want, whenever I want. The possibilities seem endless.

There's no reason to stay here any longer. There doesn't

appear to be any grand departure scheduled—no hypnotic light pulling me in. Maybe there is no heaven or hell. Could it be that when we die our spirits just wander the earth?

I guess I'll go home. No need to pack before the flight; everything stays. But why do I need to *fly* all the way home? Why can't I just beam myself around like on *Star Trek*? I focus on wanting to be at my condo and sure enough, in the blink of an eye, I'm standing in my living room. Awesome! Not only can I fly but I can teleport myself as well, two of my ultimate fantasies. They'll come in handy since I've got a lot of ground to cover. It's a big world out there and I've got to find some answers about what I'm doing here.

3

The Old Man and the Cave

Staring out my living room window, I'm mesmerized by the amazing ocean view I worked so hard to get but never really took the time to fully enjoy. I moved in here less than a year ago and much of my stuff remains in boxes sealed with packing tape.

When I was growing up, money was always in short supply, so when I started working it became an obsession to climb above the poverty line. I moved back home after graduation and made it a priority to get Mom and I out of our neighborhood as soon as possible. Throughout high school, I had the hope of signing a large pro contract after college and buying a new home for her in a better area, but that dream evaporated. It took a couple of years, but eventually we were able to relocate to a safer neighborhood and leave the anxieties of our former neighborhood behind.

Mom always worked incredibly hard. Dad died without any life insurance, which made things especially difficult on her, but she kept us afloat and allowed me to go to school and play sports without having to get a job to help support us. As soon as I was able, I made a point of insuring my life with a substantial policy and named Mom as the sole beneficiary. It's an enormous relief to know that money will help take care of her for a long time.

Wandering the neighborhood over the next couple of days, I find that life simply goes on for the living. I take a long walk along the crowded beach, visit a few local bars and restaurants, mingling unnoticed among thousands of people, but find no trace of another kindred spirit. It's estimated over 150,000 people die *every* day in this world, almost two people every second. Where in the hell is everybody? I feel totally alone while surrounded by millions of people.

I'm tired of haunting this place. SC is practicing today so I think I'll head down to the campus and see how things are shaping up after the big win against Tennessee. It will be a welcome distraction to fly around campus and check on the team as they prepare for their upcoming game against Minnesota.

The Golden Gophers have always been a respectable program and are one of the founding members of the Big Ten Conference, but they haven't been among the nation's elite or even a conference power for several decades. Their heyday was back in the 1930s and early '40s when they won five national championships and were one of college football's great dynasties. Football legend Bronko Nagurski was a consensus All-American at Minnesota. Even though Minnesota football has been out of the national spotlight for quite some time, they're a legitimate non-conference opponent for USC, which has always strived to play solid competition outside of its Pac-12 schedule.

Soaring over SC's campus, I can't help but think about how

unique this place is. An illustrious, private university located in the center of LA's sprawling metropolis—The Entertainment Capital of the World. By contrast, most of college football's other elite programs are based in smaller cities or college towns and in many cases are literally the only game in town. Even though the locations of these great powerhouses vary widely, one thing doesn't change. Passion for our favorite college football teams runs very deep everywhere you go across America.

Football practice has started, and I hover like a drone over the field. Coaches are barking out their instructions and players are going through their various position drills. The mood and energy around the team is focused and intense as expectations for this season are lofty as usual. They begin the final eleven-on-eleven scrimmage of the day and I move down to the sidelines for a closer look. The level of play is extremely physical, and the pads are popping. You don't need to see a hit to know if it's good; you can hear it. Players are going all out, as the competition for playing time is fierce.

Someone on the far side of the field catches my attention. He's an older fellow and there's something a little different about him. Looking in my direction he begins to wave. Can this guy actually see me? I keep my eye on him and he's motioning for me to come over. I point to myself like, "Are you waving at me?" He nods and continues to wave. I don't want to freak him out by flying so I walk over to him.

"Hiya, pal," he says. "Harold's the name."

"How can you see me?" I ask.

"I'm a ghost just like you. Welcome to the afterlife."

"Thanks. My name is Kyle. You have no idea how glad I am to see you. I was beginning to think I was the only ghost wandering the earth."

"Nope, there aren't many, but you're not alone. I get down here pretty regularly myself. I heard about your accident and came down to meet you. Choked on a hot dog, huh? Was there anybody around to help you?"

"No, I was alone. Tried to give myself the Heimlich but it didn't work. I started to cut open my windpipe with a steak knife, but I passed out and ended up cutting my throat."

"Wow! Sorry to hear that. You're a young man. That's a tough way to go."

"How did you die?" I ask.

"I was fortunate, had a long life, died when I was eighty-seven. I had Parkinson's, was in the hospital for a long time near the end, pneumonia finally got me. I was married to my beautiful wife for forty-nine years, no children." He pauses. "You seem like a nice kid, Kyle. Why don't I show you around?"

Practice had ended a while ago and we were the only ones left on the field except for a few seagulls circling overhead. "Sounds good, where do we start?"

"Follow me," he says and with the snap of his fingers we're gone.

Instantly, we're transported to an amazing cavern. The

place is enormous and fully equipped with all the comforts you could ever want. A beautiful, dark wood bar with a highly polished brass railing sits along one wall, completely stocked to rival any of the best watering holes on earth. Antique gas lamps light the place throughout. There's a huge fireplace with a roaring fire, giant flat screen TVs, pool table, poker table, plush leather sofas and chairs. Memorabilia is all over the walls. "Wow, this is awesome!"

"Welcome to the man cave," says Harold.

"I'm surprised you ever leave," I reply.

"Got to get out and keep tabs on the real world, my boy. What'll you have to drink?"

"I didn't think ghosts drank," I respond.

"We don't *need* to drink or even eat for that matter," he replies, "but we can pretty much do whatever we want here so why not enjoy some of the simple pleasures of life?"

"Okay, I'll have whatever you're having."

"Excellent. Rye whiskey on the rocks it is." Harold calls out, "Oh Belvedere!" Out of nowhere a grayish, elderly looking gentleman dressed in a butler's uniform shuffles over. "Belvedere, I'd like you to meet our new friend Kyle."

With a vintage Southern accent, he responds, "Hello Mr. Kyle, pleased to meet you."

"Likewise, Belvedere, the pleasure's all mine."

"What will you gentlemen be having?"

"Two rye whiskeys on the rocks please, Belvedere," Harold

says giving me a nudge. "I love saying his name. Belvedere just kind of rolls off the tongue doesn't it?" He walks over to a couple of large, overstuffed leather chairs by the fireplace and opens a humidor sitting on the table. "Have a seat Kyle. Would you care for a cigar?"

"Okay, thanks. I don't smoke but what the heck. I don't have to worry about my health anymore." Belvedere brings the drinks over and lights my cigar. "So, tell me, what is this place?"

"This is my home base. Pretty special, huh?"

"Is this all real?"

"It's as real as you want it to be. We create our own reality here; might as well enjoy ourselves in the process."

"This place reminds me of when I was a young kid. When I was growing up, I would hear about game days at Notre Dame. They would say that the students and alumni would make their way over to the Grotto before kickoff. I wasn't familiar with Catholic traditions, so I figured the Grotto has to be a popular bar or hangout. What a great name for a campus saloon. I envisioned it to be much like this cavern; everyone heads over there before the game for a little Irish cheer and liquid fortification. Little did I know the Grotto is not a barroom, but a sacred place to light candles and pray."

"Hilarious! I love it." Harold bursts out laughing. He stands and raises his glass. "I hereby christen this place the Grotto in honor of my new pal Kyle."

"By the way, where are we? Is this heaven?"

"No, this is purgatory. We're in between heaven and earth."

"How do people end up here?"

"Purgatory is a place where spirits go before they're ready to enter the great beyond. It's kind of like a finishing school for heaven. Those souls have some issues they need to resolve before they can move on. When people die, most either get called directly to heaven or else they end up here in purgatory. The really bad ones get sent downstairs to spend eternity on the wrong end of a pitchfork."

"Why am I here?" I ask.

"I can't answer that Kyle. That's something you'll have to discover for yourself. I do know that you love football and that's one of the main reasons I came down to meet you. I'm here because I love the game as well. When I died, I had lived a long life. I was happy and successful, but I couldn't leave the game behind. It meant everything to me, it was in my blood. I had a calling to stay behind and watch over the game. So here I am."

"Judging from your setup here, purgatory doesn't seem too bad."

"I've been given a unique role in this domain and the Grotto is a special place. I'll be here until I'm ready to hang up my cleats and move on," he says.

"For now, you're welcome to stay here, relax, and enjoy the Grotto. I need to leave for a while to visit an old friend. I won't be gone long. Belvedere is always here. Just call out and he'll bring you anything you want."

And with that Harold vanishes.

4

The Ghost

I wander around the Grotto and shoot some pool to pass the time. Finishing my drink, I call out for Belvedere to get a refill and he immediately appears.

"Yes Mr. Kyle, how can I help you?"

"How about another rye on the rocks?"

"Very good sir. Will there be anything else?"

"What do you recommend?"

"May I suggest our specialty of the house, a prime porterhouse steak dinner with all the trimmings."

"That sounds delicious, medium rare please." A few minutes later he returns with the most wonderful smelling, sizzling steak dinner. I sit down and devour the best steak I have ever eaten.

Curious about my new host I ask, "Belvedere, how long have you known Harold?"

"Quite some time sir, ever since the day he died. We both passed away at the same time. He was in the hospital in Florida and I died at my employer's home in Savannah. Our souls were drawn together, and they asked us if we would like to stay behind. When he agreed, I couldn't refuse the opportunity to stay and attend to him."

"Who asked you both to stay?"

"Why the angels, sir."

"I didn't see any angels when I died."

"No, if you're supposed to be in limbo the angels don't come for you. Nothing much happens when you die. They just kind of leave you hanging on earth."

"Why did you want to stay behind, Belvedere?"

"I've been a servant my entire life as was my father and his father before him. This is all I've ever known. It's all I ever wanted to do, and it makes me happy. They also said if I ever got tired and wanted to leave, the gates of heaven would always be open for me. So why not stay behind, do what I love and be of service to an important man like Mr. Red?"

"Harold's last name is Red?"

"No Mr. Kyle, Red is his nickname. His full name is Harold Edward Grange."

"Wait a minute! You mean Harold is Red Grange, the Galloping Ghost?"

"Yes sir. He is indeed."

"I can't believe this! I'm hanging out with Red Grange, the greatest college football player of all time. The most famous ghost in sports history. I had no idea; I didn't recognize him."

"Mr. Red died when he was eighty-seven years old, so he doesn't quite look like he did in his playing days back in the twenties and thirties. Will you be having anything else, Mr. Kyle?"

"Hang on, Belvedere. Red played a long time ago, several

decades before I was born. What can you tell me about him before you go?"

"I think Ms. Jessica would be best suited to help you with that, Mr. Kyle. She can tell you everything you want to know about Mr. Red." He calls out, "Ms. Jessica, would you be so kind as to help our new friend here?"

"Certainly, Belvedere, my pleasure," a woman's voice answers, but no one appears. "Hello Kyle, it's nice to meet you."

"Pleased to meet you, Jessica, but where are you? I don't see you anywhere."

"I'm here; I just don't have a human form."

"Jessica is one of our angels," says Belvedere. "She knows Mr. Red better than he knows himself. I'll leave you two now. Let me know if you need anything, Mr. Kyle."

"Jessica, I'd like to know more about Red's career. Can you tell me about him?"

"Of course, I can tell you anything you want to know, but I can do even better than that," she says, as an antique movie projector appears and the Grotto falls into darkness. The machine whirls to life, flickering old-time newsreel images on a big screen.

The film's announcer booms out, "Movietone Presents Red Grange, the Galloping Ghost—An American Legend."

I look around for a chair to pull up and Jessica asks if I'm ready. "Yes ma'am," I reply.

"Hold on!" she says as a thrust of light from the silver screen reaches out and grabs me, pulling me into the film's black-and-white world.

I've often wondered what it would be like to be in the movies and now I'm actually inside of one. It's a roller coaster of a ride as the newsreel cuts from one gridiron clip to another, showing a twentysomething Grange running roughshod against overmatched opponents. I'm in the middle of the action, witnessing everything as it happened nearly a hundred years ago.

The announcer continues, "Harold 'Red' Grange is one of the greatest football players in history, considered by many to be the best college football player of all time."

I watch Red play in his first varsity game as a sophomore at the University of Illinois. He breaks loose on runs of sixty, thirty-five, and twelve yards scoring all three of the Fighting Illini's touchdowns in a 24–7 season opening victory over Nebraska. His speed, elusiveness and toughness make him an instant star. He goes on to lead Illinois to an undefeated season and a share of the 1923 national championship.

At the end of the season, Walter Camp, the "Father of American Football," steps up to a press conference podium to announce his All-America team and names Grange to the squad, describing him as "not only a line smasher of great power, but also a sterling open field runner—one of the most dangerous men in the country."

The film cuts to the following season as Grange and the Illini square off against powerhouse Michigan. The Wolverines haven't lost a game in three years and shared the national title last year with Illinois.

Red quickly turns the game into a rout, taking the opening kickoff back ninety-five yards for a score. He follows that up with three more touchdowns, all within the game's first twelve minutes. Grange adds another rushing touchdown in the third quarter and finishes off the scoring by throwing an eighteen-yard touchdown pass in the final period. Red and Illinois dominate Michigan 39–14. Grange's six touchdowns total more points than Michigan has allowed in the previous two seasons combined.

Up in the press box, sportswriters are frantically tapping out their accounts of the historic game. Everyone's grasping for colorful superlatives to describe the country's brightest new star. Warren Brown with the *Chicago Herald-Examiner* comes up with the most memorable, nicknaming Grange "The Galloping Ghost."

A group of reporters is gathered around legendary coach Amos Alonzo Stagg, who calls Grange's effort "the most spectacular, single-handed performance ever delivered in a major game."

The announcer chimes in, "The Golden Age of Sports made legends out of Babe Ruth, Jack Dempsey and Bobby Jones, but none were more famous than Red Grange, who brought college football into the mainstream of American life."

A rapid procession of swirling newspapers that freeze in succession fill the screen with bold headlines touting Grange's exploits. It concludes with a portrait of Red on the cover of *Time* magazine.

"Even with all that notoriety," the announcer says, "there remains some skepticism about Grange in the East where college football's Ivy League power structure still resides. When Illinois plays at the University of Pennsylvania on October 31, 1925, Grange will have the opportunity to silence any remaining doubters."

Penn is a power in the East, one of the best teams in the United States and heavily favored to beat the struggling Illini. Illinois has gotten off to a slow start this season, dropping three of their first four games due to the loss of several key players to graduation and injuries. Red was moved to quarterback after the third game of the season and was forced to learn the new position on the fly.

The weather in Philadelphia has been miserable leading up to the game. It rained and snowed most of the night before. By game time it is still cold and wet, but that doesn't stop the 65,000 fans from filling Franklin Field. The field is a swampy mess of ankle-deep mud.

In the weeks prior to the game, Illinois' coach, Bob Zuppke, finds a vulnerability in Penn's defense he thinks he can exploit. The Quakers have a tendency to heavily overload their defense to the opponent's strong side leaving the weak side virtually unguarded.

Zuppke instructs Red to run their first two plays directly

into the teeth of Penn's stacked defense. The plays go nowhere, but they set Illinois up for their next possession. On the first snap, Grange takes the ball around the weak side and sprints uncontested fifty-five yards for the game's first score. While the players on both teams are noticeably bogged down by the sloppy conditions, Red seems unfazed, running and cutting as if it were a dry field of freshly mowed turf.

Zuppke's offensive strategy continues to work throughout the first half as Illinois scores two more touchdowns, one by Grange on a twelve-yard run. The teams go into halftime with Illinois leading Penn 18–2.

Penn adjusts its defense in the second half, but it can't stop the Ghost on one last jaw-dropping play. Illinois is driving down to Penn's twenty-yard line and Grange decides to call some razzle-dazzle. They line up in field goal formation with Red kneeling down eight yards behind center to hold for kicker Earl Britton. The center snaps the ball but, instead of going to Grange, it goes directly back to Britton who tosses a short pass to Chuck Kassel at right end. Kassel then turns around and flips a lateral to Grange running around the right end. Penn's stunned defense offers no resistance; Grange takes it all the way in for the game's final score.

"Red Grange and Illinois pummel Penn into surrender, 24–2," the announcer declares. "The Galloping Ghost has one of his finest collegiate games running for three hundred sixty-three yards and three touchdowns. The East is convinced.

Damon Runyon writes, 'This man Red Grange of Illinois is three or four men and a horse rolled into one for football purposes. He is Jack Dempsey, Babe Ruth, Al Jolson, Paavo Nurmi and Man o' War. Put them all together, they spell Grange.'

Three weeks later, Red plays his final game for Illinois and declares that he is leaving school to turn pro, joining the Chicago Bears. We're in a suite in the Morrison Hotel in Chicago where Red is seated at a table next to his manager, C.C. Pyle, and the owners of the Bears, George Halas and Dutch Sternamen. The room is swarming with reporters and photographers jockeying to get a glimpse of the historic moment. The announcer says, "Red Grange signs a contract with the Chicago Bears that will pay him the astronomical sum of one hundred thousand dollars for his first season in professional football. The Galloping Ghost and his new team will embark on a grueling national tour, playing nineteen games over the next two months."

Fans pack stadiums across the country to watch the legend from Illinois and his Chicago teammates introduce America to the fledgling National Football League.

We jump to Chicago where Red is in his third season playing out the final minute of a lost game. He goes up to haul in a pass against a defender and the collision causes his cleats to catch in the turf. I hear a sickening crunch and snap as his knee grotesquely twists from the impact. The Ghost lies on the field unable to get up. His teammates eventually help him off the field. The announcer says, "Red Grange sustains a serious knee injury that could derail his career. His valiant attempts to play the rest of the year are not encouraging and he misses all of the following season. Have we seen the last of the Galloping Ghost?"

Red's knee is never the same. His ability to cut laterally is gone forever. Thinking his career is over, he is ultimately coaxed out of retirement to rejoin the Bears and discovers he can still be a strong, straight-ahead runner. Upon his return I see a different type of player in Grange, no longer the elusive ghost, but still a great athlete and valuable contributor.

"Red Grange makes a successful return to the gridiron after his devastating injury," says the announcer. "Despite his limitations, he is still one of the best players in the NFL and goes on to play five more years for the Bears before ending his Hall of Fame career in 1934."

The newsreel concludes with a cut to the late 1970s. We're at the Bears headquarters watching Chris Berman of ESPN interview George Halas.

Berman asks Halas, "Who is the greatest running back you ever saw?"

"That would be Red Grange," Halas replies.

Berman follows up, "If Grange was playing today, how many yards do you think he'd gain?"

"About seven hundred and fifty, maybe eight hundred yards," says Halas.

Berman counters, "Well, eight hundred yards is just okay."

Halas replies, "Son, you must remember one thing. Red Grange is seventy-five years old."

5

Fireside Chat

As the last frame of the film flutters through the projector, the movie screen pushes me back out into the Grotto. The lights come back on and Red is standing there with his arms folded and a grin on his face.

"It looks like someone let the cat out of the bag," he says.

"Red, why didn't you tell him who you are?" asks Jessica.

"Who knows if anyone would recognize my name these days or even care? Besides, for an avid football fan like Kyle, I thought it might be a nice surprise for him when he did find out."

"It's a tremendous honor, Mr. Grange. You're one of the greatest figures in sports history."

"Please call me Red. It's good to hear I haven't been completely forgotten."

"Far from it sir, I mean Red. Your impact on the game is incredible."

"I'm glad you were able to meet Jessica. She's been looking out for me my whole life. I never knew her when I was alive, but I always sensed someone was watching out for me. When I passed on, I was finally able to meet her and thank her for everything she's done for me. I guess she'll be around as long as she still wants to put up with me."

"I'm always here for you Red," Jessica adds.

"In fact, Jessica and some of the other angels have been keeping an eye on you as well over the years. They knew you were destined to end up here and they've been telling me about you for a long time."

"Jessica, are you able to tell me why I'm in purgatory?" I ask.

"Unfortunately, I am not in on the master plan," she says. "You can think of us angels kind of like scouts. We watch over people, act as guides and messengers, but we don't give the orders. There's so much in our world that's incomprehensible, it's impossible for any of us, even angels, to see the grand scheme. Sometimes, something we see as a tragedy, like you dying at such a young age, will turn out later to be a blessing in disguise. In time, you'll discover your fate."

"Why don't we go have a seat over by the fire, Kyle," says Red. "How's your drink? I know I could use one. Oh Belvedere!"

"While you were out, Belvedere set me up with the best steak dinner I've ever had and I didn't choke to death."

"That's good to hear," Red laughs. "Belvedere really knows how to take care of people." He stokes the fire and adds another log. "I understand you were quite a football player growing up. I was sorry to hear you weren't able to play in college. What happened?"

"It was a scary situation and a tough break," I reply. "I really had some lousy luck."

My mind wanders back just before the start of my freshman season. We were finishing an intense practice leading up to our first game. It's close to a hundred degrees out on the field and the sky has that blackish-brown haze of late-August smog. We're running gassers and I'm pushing myself as hard as I can. My chest starts hurting and it gets harder to breathe. I'm thinking it's got to be the smog, but suddenly my body just gives out and I'm bent over in exhaustion. My chest is killing me like I'm being stabbed in the heart and I can't catch my breath. Gasping for air, I rip off my helmet and take a knee. My heart is in overdrive, pounding erratically like it's trying to bust out of my chest. I hear whistles blow and a trainer comes over. He asks what's going on but I can't get any words out. "Lay down and try to relax," he says.

Flat on my back, I'm surrounded by players and coaches looking down at me with worried stares and then everything goes dark. I hear someone shout, "Call 9-1-1!"

Eventually, I wake to the sound of a siren and struggle to open my eyes. Strapped to a gurney, I'm sucking air through a mask in the back of an ambulance flying through traffic. The next thing I remember, I'm in intensive care and I hear my mom talking on her cell; her voice is noticeably shaky.

"He's been in here for several hours now," she says. "They've been running all kinds of tests and we're waiting to hear what's going on."

A doctor walks into the room looking through a file. "Kyle,

you're a very lucky young man," he says. "You had a cardiac arrest at practice."

"Aren't I a little young to have a heart attack?"

"It was more than a heart attack. Your heart stopped. Technically, you were dead for a brief period of time. The good news is you're alive and you beat some pretty incredible odds. Very few people survive a cardiac arrest outside of the hospital."

"Do you know why this happened?" Mom asks.

"We've run a full battery of tests and found that Kyle has a condition known as myocarditis. It's a disease that causes inflammation of the heart muscle. It can be caused by a viral infection, among other things, but sometimes we don't know what causes it."

"How soon before I can start playing again?"

"I'm afraid it's going to be quite a while before we can even think about starting you on any kind of exercise program. You're going to be on a complete restriction from all competitive sports for the next three to six months. Unfortunately, any thought of playing this season is completely out of the question. You've had a very serious episode, Kyle. You need to be thankful you're alive. For now, we need you to focus on getting plenty of rest and giving your heart a chance to recover."

The next several months crawled by. Missing my freshman season was excruciating. Sitting in an exam room at the cardiologist's office, Mom and I nervously wait for the doctor, hoping for some good news. The doctor comes in and I try to read his face for some clues. I can tell something's not right.

"Kyle, we've been checking your progress routinely over the past six months and regrettably your heart hasn't responded as we would have hoped. It sustained a significant amount of damage which caused scarring to a large part of the organ. Many times, when a patient is diagnosed with myocarditis, rest and medication allow the heart to heal and make a full recovery. However, in your case, you have a chronic condition that puts you at greater risk of arrhythmias and sudden cardiac death. This means that a return to competitive sports is not possible; the risks are simply too great. With proper care though, you should be able to live a relatively normal life."

His words just hang in the air. The disappointment washes over me like a shockwave as tears well up in my eyes. Mom reaches over to hug me. "It's going to be okay. We'll get through this," she whispers.

"I'm sorry, Kyle," he says. "I wish I had better news. I would encourage you to get other opinions to make sure you're satisfied with our recommendations."

In the months that followed I sought out other specialists. If this meant the end of my playing career, I wasn't going down without a fight. Sadly, all their conclusions came back the same. It was over. I loved playing football so much I felt like I would die for the sport, but when it truly became a matter of life and death, I had no choice. It was time to move on.

"I feel your pain, Kyle," says Red. "When I tore up my

knee, I thought my career was over. I had a difficult time thinking about life after football. It was depressing."

"Ever since football was taken away, I've had a gnawing emptiness in my life. I never found another true passion to pursue. It's been a bitter disappointment."

"That may have something to do with how you ended up in purgatory. God works in mysterious ways," says Red. "What did you do to bounce back?" he asks.

"I still had my scholarship so I focused on getting my degree and, a few months before graduation, one of the staffers from the athletic department suggested I come and talk to them about the possibility of working in the department doing fundraising after I finished up with school. The idea interested me and seemed like a good way to put my business major to work. I had stayed in touch with the coaches after I left the team and all of them were incredibly supportive of me working in the department. They gave me great recommendations and the opportunity seemed to click. I got the job and went right to work after graduation and was there ever since. It was a good-paying job and I did well at it, but it was a far cry from getting paid to play football for a living."

"What did you do for fun after you couldn't play anymore?" he asks.

"College football became an all-consuming hobby for me. I left the Xs and Os behind for the players and coaches and immersed myself in the history and traditions of the sport.

Most fans' obsessions revolve around their favorite team, but I wanted to know about more than just USC. There's an entire nation of great football programs out there, each with their own unique legacy. I had a photographic memory and could absorb enormous amounts of information with little effort. I could learn playbooks overnight and schoolwork was usually a breeze. I became a walking encyclopedia on college football."

"Football is the greatest sport we have, that's for sure—nothing compares," says Red. "There's so much about the game that makes it compelling. Whether you're playing, coaching or just watching, it gets under your skin and doesn't let go.

"I remember Vince Lombardi used to say, 'Football's not a contact sport, it's a collision sport. Dancing is a contact sport.' Those collisions are what we love to dish out and are a big part of what people come to see. Football is controlled, competitive violence. You need to be physically and mentally tough to play this game. It teaches you to face your fears, be strong, take a punishing hit, get back up, and come back for more."

"When you think about it, football's a pretty simple game for people to pick up and watch," I say. "You can keep track of the quarterback, running backs and receivers to see what they do with the ball. They either move it downfield and score or they don't. The defense reads and reacts to the offense and either stops them or not. But what I love is the complexity involved to make everything work. It's unlike any other sport. There are eleven guys on both sides of the ball and each player has a specific assignment on every single play that's designed to accomplish a certain outcome. The strategy, teamwork and execution required to make everything work ultimately determines a team's success or failure.

"Another thing that makes the game so captivating is that every game matters. Baseball and basketball have long seasons with lots of games. Football is such a physically demanding sport that you have shorter seasons and a much more limited number of games. Each contest is a major event. Fans tailgating for hours before kickoff, cavernous stadiums packed with huge crowds. The action on the field along with the bands and cheerleaders generates incredible excitement. The roar of a crowd reacting to a big play causes a huge rush of adrenaline."

"Also, in college football, every game matters even more," Red says. "There's no preseason in college football, and its regular season is the best in all of sports. Every contest is essentially a playoff game. There's no opportunity to play any practice games to work out the kinks and calm the jitters. The margin for error during the regular season is razor thin. Only four teams out of one hundred thirty in major college football qualify for the College Football Playoff. A school's national championship hopes can take a serious hit with just one loss, even if it's in the first week of the season. The four best teams at the end of the year are determined by their body of work over the course of the season, and you must be near perfect all season long to have a shot at the national championship. A team that loses a couple of games early in the year, but then goes on to win the rest of their games, may end up being one of the best teams in the nation at the end of the regular season. However, they have little chance at making the final four over an undefeated or one-loss team.

"Pro football has a preseason to iron things out and decide who's going to make their rosters. The NFL regular season is important, but there is much more room for error in pro ball since almost forty percent of the teams in the league qualify for the playoffs."

"Talk about room for error," I say. "How about the Seattle Seahawks making the playoffs in 2010 after going 7-9 in the regular season or the Carolina Panthers qualifying in 2014 at 7-8-1?"

"Yep, in pro ball you can have a mediocre season but get hot at the end, make the playoffs and even reach the Super Bowl. You remember the 2011 New York Giants *winning* the Super Bowl after going 9-7? No college team in America would have any chance of competing for a national championship after losing almost half its regular season games."

"Which do you like better, college or pro?" I ask.

"College football is absolutely my favorite," says Red. "The NFL is the highest level of the sport with the best players, but it is strictly a business and there's no room for amateurs. They say the NFL stands for Not For Long because if you don't have what it takes, you're gone. Also, college teams don't pick up and move like what you experienced in Los Angeles with the

Rams and Raiders. Universities are entrenched where they are, so you don't have to worry about losing your team to another city, unlike pro teams who'll pick up and leave in pursuit of a better deal despite the fans they leave behind."

"The college ranks are unique in so many ways," I add. "For one thing, it's not a level playing field. The NFL, like most pro sports leagues, goes to great lengths to create parity within their ranks for the sake of competitive balance. Things like salary caps and college drafts are designed to boost weaker teams and help create a level playing field. In college, the rich and powerful programs have more advantages to maintain their power structure. From a talent standpoint schools are free to recruit and enroll any athlete that meets their qualifications. They can go after and sign as many top players as they're able to, provided they don't exceed the mandated twenty-five scholarship limit in any given year. The best programs typically get the lion's share of the best players, year in and year out.

"Plus, I really like the variety in college football. There are many different types of offenses being run at the college level, which makes it more interesting and unpredictable. I think it leads to more big plays. Much of the innovation in the game comes from the college and high school levels. The NFL is more homogeneous and conservative across the league. Colleges, more often, are playing to win games, whereas the NFL leans more toward trying not to lose them. Colleges are more likely to go for it on fourth down rather than kick a field goal.

The NFL is more likely to take the three points and move on."

Red lights a cigar and pauses a moment. "Another big reason for my devotion to college football are the student-athletes playing at the highest amateur level of the sport for the love of the game and pride for their team and school. Sure, some of them are trying to grab the brass ring and make it to the NFL, but the overwhelming majority will never play another game after they leave college. Fewer than two percent of the kids that play college football make it to the pros. It takes a tremendous amount of desire to play in college. The hard work year-round and the sacrifices you need to make really show how much you love the game."

"Of course, one of the main things that sets college football apart from everything else are the incredible traditions," I say. "College football, without its traditions, is like watching the NFL. Some of the best memories of my life are the marching bands, the fight songs, the cheerleaders, the mascots, the rivalries, the bowl games and definitely, the tailgating. I'm really going to miss all of that."

"I know what you mean," laments Red. But after a moment he jumps out of his chair and says, "Hey, you don't have to miss it just yet. Let's make the most of the time you're here. We've got to get you out and have some fun. You know what you need? A road trip!"

6

Road Trip

Red snaps his fingers and soon we're gliding over the University of Mississippi campus in Oxford. The Grove at Ole Miss is a huge, ten-acre, tree-filled area in the middle of campus that's packed on game days with tents, fans, food and drinks in a sea of red and blue—one of the best tailgates in America. "There have gotta be a hundred thousand people here today," I say, "but where are all the cars?"

"Cars haven't been allowed in The Grove since 1991 when a whopper of a storm temporarily turned the place into a swamp," Red says. "It's been a tent city ever since."

We perch ourselves like Huck Finn and Tom Sawyer on the branches of an old magnolia tree and check out the massive gathering.

Someone in the crowd below shouts out, "Are you ready?" and right on cue a large pack of Rebel fans answer back.

"Hell yeah! Damn right!
Hotty Toddy, gosh almighty,
Who the hell are we? Hey!
Flim flam, bim bam
Ole Miss, by damn!"

The group howls their approval afterward.

"I love that cheer!" I shout. "I've got to find out what Hotty Toddy means."

"Don't bother," says Red. "Rebel fans don't really know either. But whatever it is, it means the world to them. They use it as a greeting and whenever someone in Oxford calls out 'Are you ready?' the Hotty Toddy cheer is the answer."

Red gazes out over the enormous celebration and wonders aloud, "When do you suppose this whole idea of tailgating first got started?"

"Some think it was at the first intercollegiate football game ever played back in 1869 between Rutgers and Princeton," I reply. "On the other hand, Harvard and Yale claim they started the tradition at their game in 1906. However, the early origins of these types of gatherings go a lot farther back in history. The Reign of Terror during the French Revolution had a tailgate-like atmosphere. People would bring their families together to eat, drink and be merry before watching the guillotine executions of thousands of their fellow countrymen. Here in America, a precursor to tailgating took place during the first major battle of the Civil War. In 1861, at the First Battle of Bull Run, spectators gathered with picnic baskets, blankets, food, and drinks to witness the bloodshed and root for their favorite side. The underdog Gray squad routed the heavily favored Blue that day, kicking off the deadliest war in American history."

"Wow, that's pretty impressive, Kyle. You really know your stuff."

"Like I said earlier, when I couldn't play football anymore, I had a lot of free time on my hands."

"Things have really changed since the early days of picnic baskets and blankets," says Red. "Nowadays, tailgating has been raised to an elaborate art form with mammoth-sized RVs and tent cities with deluxe grills and smokers, flat screen TVs, satellite dishes, generators and extravagant spreads of food and drinks. The parties get going hours, even days before kickoff and are so popular that about a third of the tailgaters don't even go inside to the game."

The irresistible aroma of fried chicken, ribs, burgers and brats swirling through the air hypnotically pulls us down from our perch and we begin to stroll among the crowd.

"I'm parched," says Red. "Time for a super-sized beer and something to eat."

Moving from tent to tent, our imaginations allow us to help ourselves to the local cuisine. Lavish spreads of food and drinks are laid out in canopies decorated in cardinal red and navy blue and adorned with chandeliers, candelabras, lace doilies and fine china. People with red cups filled with their favorite beverages are everywhere.

"Food is one of my favorite hobbies and we can eat all we want," says Red. "I make it a point to get down to earth regularly and visit tailgates across the country."

"What are some of your favorites?"

"While I'm down on the Bayou, I love their Cajun and Creole cooking. LSU fans serve up some mouth-watering gumbo and jambalaya. When they play Florida, grilled alligator is usually on the menu. I think it tastes like chicken. You never know what you'll come across. Over in Arkansas they grill up pieces of crow meat and jalapeno wrapped in bacon—yum! In Texas they have a dish called beef barbacoa de cabeza."

"Wait, is that what I think it is?" I ask.

"Yep, they take an entire steer head, slow-roast it and serve it up on a platter. It's the perfect finger food: you just pull the meat like tongue and cheek right off the skull. The tacos are delicious. At Central Florida, I've had whole smoked armadillo served right in its own shell. If you like seafood, head up to the Pacific Northwest. Washington fans dish up fresh salmon, lobster and oysters while *sailgating* on their boats docked in the bay right outside Husky Stadium."

"I'm stuffed from all this food talk; we gotta keep moving." I conjure up a couple of red cups filled with ice-cold beer and we continue to meander among the crowd. Along the way, we overhear a loyal Rebels fan mourning the misfortunes of Ole Miss football to his friend. "Well, our team hasn't been very good and we may not win the game, but we always win the party," he says.

We spot some fans playing cornhole and Red says he'd like to give it a try, so we fantasize our own cornhole setup and start warming up. The Ghost is having trouble even hitting the board with a beanbag. After he comes up empty with several attempts, I suggest, "Maybe we should play beer pong instead."

"Very funny, I'm just getting warmed up," he says. "Okay, hotshot, let's make it interesting. How about a friendly wager?"

"Really?" I'm thinking this should be like shooting fish in a barrel. "What do you have in mind?"

"The loser has to carry the winner around the Grove on his shoulders for the rest of the day," he says.

"Sounds ridiculous, but okay, you're on." I go first and toss an ace, stopping the bag just a few inches from the hole. Red throws a slider, landing it in front of the hole and slipping it in.

"Cornhole!" he shouts.

Hmmm, that's got to be a fluke. I line up for my next toss, which drops for a hanger just barely on the edge of the hole.

"Nice try. Close, but no cigar," he says. Grange takes his next toss and lofts a perfect spinner that sails straight through the hole. "Swish! Nothin' but corn!" he hollers and starts strutting a funky celebration dance. That toss was no fluke.

"You set me up you sandbagger. You couldn't even hit the board when we were warming up."

Red laughs, "It's just beginner's luck."

We keep playing, but no matter what I try, my throws just won't go down. Meanwhile, Grange is putting on a clinic, sinking nearly everything he tosses up.

"Okay Red, what's your secret?"

"Kyle, I like you and I'm gonna give you a little advice. You see, there's a force in the universe that makes things happen and all you have to do is get in touch with it. Stop thinking, let things happen, and be the beanbag."

"Shut up! Like I haven't seen *Caddyshack.*" Red starts laughing as I'm pelting him with beanbags. "Cornhole this!" I say.

A bet's a bet, however, and I eventually kneel down and tell the Ghost to saddle up on my shoulders. He tries to beg off the wager, but I insist. We shuffle our way through the crowd as Red howls out the Illinois fight song in between hiccups; I think he's been overserved. I feel pretty goofy and I know this must look absurd, but I wish I had a picture of us. It's not every day you get to carry a legend on your shoulders.

"This has to be one of the best-dressed tailgates I've ever seen," I remark. Many of the fans are clad in their Sunday best. Lots of the women are in dresses and several of the men are in sport coats and ties.

"It reminds me of when I played," Red says. "People used to spruce up to go to games. Women in dresses and hats. Men in suits, ties and hats."

"I'm struck by how polite and friendly people are, even to fans from the other team. It's a very hospitable environment."

"We're in the heart of the Deep South here," Red says. "Manners and hospitality are the order of the day."

It's a couple of hours before kickoff and the crowd begins to part like the Red Sea. Everyone is cheering as the Rebels football team makes their Walk of Champions right through the middle of this gigantic gathering on their way to the stadium. We're surrounded by people and I can't see a thing, but the Ghost is cheering on the team from his bird's-eye view. "You sure you can see okay from up there?" I ask.

"Yep, you're doing a great job, pal, but you can let me down now. It's time to move on."

"Where are we going?" I ask.

"Boulder, Colorado," he says, snapping his fingers.

In a flash we're at Folsom Field before the start of the game between the Colorado Buffaloes and the Utah Utes, a rivalry game known as the Rumble in the Rockies.

"I've got a surprise for you," Red says. "You're going to run out on the field with the Colorado team before kickoff."

"Okay, that sounds pretty cool."

"You're actually going to be out in front leading the team," Red says, pausing for effect. "Aboard Ralphie the Buffalo."

"Now we're talking!"

Ralphie's Run is one of the most exciting traditions in college football. Ralphie is the school's live mascot, a 1,200-pound bison. CU has been running Ralphie at games since 1967 and they're on number five now, all females.

Ralphie's in a pen on the field in front of the team's entrance. The players have come out of the locker room and are gathered behind her waiting to take the field. Red and I approach her and say hello. She knows we're here; animals can sense us. I ask her if it would be all right if I hitch a ride and she lets me know to climb aboard. I jump in the pen and settle on top of the enormous animal and get a firm grip on her harness. There are five handlers outside the pen; each has a rope fastened to her harness ready to make the run with her. I've seen this before on TV and I know this animal can really move. The gate to the pen opens as the stadium announcer shouts, "Here comes Ralphie!" The crowd roars as she takes off in a full gallop down the field. I am holding on for dear life. As she reaches the opposite end of the field the handlers guide her through the turn and into the final 100-yard sprint to the finish. Like a racehorse heading down the homestretch, Ralphie kicks it into high gear and we are flying. The handlers are racing full speed alongside us and as we reach the end, her open trailer awaits and she runs straight inside. "Wow, what a ride! I feel like a kid at Disneyland. What's next?" I ask.

"Let's head over to Berkeley, California," says Red. "I've always wanted to check out the view from Tightwad Hill."

Snap!

We're high up on a hill overlooking Cal's Memorial Stadium. I've been to several games here in the past and have always seen the people perched up here.

Tightwad Hill, officially called Charter Hill, was created from the dirt excavated from Strawberry Canyon when they built Memorial Stadium in 1923. Students and fans have been coming up to this diehard Cal rooting spot since they opened the stadium, mainly because they couldn't afford the tickets and the hill offered an unobstructed view of the field free of charge. It can be a little treacherous to get up here, but the regulars feel it's worth the effort because the price is right, and you can also drink booze here, which is not allowed inside the stadium.

It's a crystal-clear day and the view is spectacular. From up here you can look out over the bay and see the city of San Francisco, Alcatraz Island, and the Golden Gate Bridge. The setting is awesome; we sit back, relax, take in the game, and soak up the scenery.

"This place is definitely a unique tradition and that's what makes college football so amazing," says Red. "Traditions get us charged up when we see our team take the field before kick-off. They give us chills when we hear our school's fight song or bring a tear to our eye when they play our alma mater."

"Traditions also connect people to the past by carrying on the same rituals and customs that have been handed down for generations," I add. "They give people a sense of comfort and belonging, something they can depend on year after year. Traditions bond people together with a strong group identity and a shared mission. They're as much a part of college football as the game itself."

The Cal Band is on the field performing at halftime which reminds me, "Did you know the oldest college marching band in the country started way back in 1845 at Notre Dame? It wasn't until forty-two years later, 1887, that the Band of the

Fighting Irish had their first performance at a football game."

"You're obviously a big trivia buff," says Red. "Well, here's one for you. My alma mater's band, the Marching Illini, was the first to ever perform a halftime show at a college football game back in 1907."

Cal's band leaves the field and the cheerleaders are waiting to lead the team out to start the second half. "Did you know cheerleading officially got its start in college football in 1898 at the University of Minnesota? It was guys only and stayed that way until 1923 when the school became the first in the country to allow girls to join in. It's surprising that female cheerleaders didn't really catch on across the country until the 1940s when men were being drafted for World War II. It opened up more opportunities for women, who now dominate the tradition."

Cal has their victory cannon up here on the hill near us and they fire it every time Cal scores. It's a high scoring game and the cannon's getting a workout. It's time for us to move on. Grange surprises me by saying he wants to go for a pony ride. I immediately think of the coin operated kiddie rides in front of the supermarket or maybe the live ponies that trudge around in a circle at the park. If we were still alive, I'd be worried that Red might have been out in the sun too long. After all, he is a gray-haired, eighty-seven-year-old. I suggest we should head back to the Grotto, so he can lie down. Red bursts out laughing.

"Very funny," he says. "I guarantee this will be the best pony ride you've ever had."

Snap!

We're at Owens Field in Norman, Oklahoma, home of the Sooners, and now I realize what Red has in mind. The ponies we're going to be riding are Boomer and Sooner, the matching white pair that pull the Sooner Schooner out on the field after every Oklahoma score.

The stadium is packed for OU's battle against the Oklahoma State Cowboys in the annual Bedlam game. The Sooners are driving for their first score and the ponies and wagon are in position at the tunnel entrance to the field getting ready to make their run. We introduce ourselves to Boomer and Sooner and they're excited for their big moment to gallop out on the field in front of a cheering crowd of 86,000 fans. The Ruf/Neks spirit squad are in charge of the wagon and these guys are armed with shotguns and wooden paddles, so you don't want to mess around with them. One is at the reins in the driver's seat and the honorary Ruf/Nek Queen is riding shotgun next to him. There is another Ruf/Nek lying on his back hanging headfirst off the rear of the wagon holding a huge red OU flag. The Sooners have just scored a touchdown, so Red and I climb on top of the ponies. Everyone's set. Oklahoma kicks the extra point; the shotguns go off and the band starts up. The field is clear and off we go. The ponies immediately break into a gallop and the Ruf/Neks are running alongside in a full sprint as the crowd roars. I look over at Red; he's howling and grinning from ear to ear. If only the people in the stadium could see what I see—one of the greatest football players who ever lived, acting like a kid again, galloping around the field having the time of his life. As we start to make the turn at mid-field, I remember the story about the time they tipped the wagon over in 1993. The Schooner came charging out on the field to celebrate a score and they took the turn too sharply. The wagon tipped over sending its occupants, including the Ruf/Neks' Queen, sprawling to the turf. The young lady undoubtedly got more exposure than she bargained for that day when her dress flew up and revealed she wasn't wearing any underwear. Today, however, the Ruf/Neks have everything under control. We make a smooth turn and race back to the tunnel. It's a low bridge and everyone's got to duck down as we go hurtling into the darkness. Boomer and Sooner come to a halt, and Red and I high-five each other. "Best damn pony ride I ever had," I shout.

"Told you so," says Red.

Oklahoma is having a big day running up the score on their rivals and we end up staying around to ride the horses several more times. We can't get enough; it's just too much fun. We feel like we're honorary Ruf/Neks for the day. We got a chance to get to know the ponies as well and thank them for the rides. Mercifully for OK State, the game finally ends. The Sooners won this one 56–10. We rode the horses eight times. Time to head back to the Grotto.

Snap!

7

Unforgiven

"It's good to be home," says Red. The fire's roaring back in the Grotto and Belvedere's got a surprise waiting for us.

"Welcome back, gentlemen. I thought you'd be hungry after your journey, so I took the liberty of preparing a little something to eat," he says.

We sit down at a formally set dinner table with a white tablecloth and Belvedere lifts the sterling silver cover to reveal Lobster Thermidor, which looks mouthwatering and smells fantastic.

"Belvedere, you've outdone yourself," says Red.

"It's my pleasure sir," he replies, as he brings over a couple of cocktails.

"Cheers," says Red. "Here's to a great day!"

As I'm gorging myself on lobster, I glance around the Grotto and can't help but ask Red, "How did you ever dream this place up?"

He hesitates for a moment and says, "Well, I always wanted a swanky retreat of my own when I was alive, but I never had one, so I created this place. It kind of reminds me of my father."

"How's that?"

"After my first year in the pros, I bought a house for him

and we set up a den on the third floor; it became one of his favorite places. We furnished it with all the comforts you see here in the Grotto. He'd have all his old friends over and they'd while away the hours telling tales and playing cards.

"When I died, the man cave phenomenon was becoming a popular notion, so I thought, what could be better than the real thing? I came up with this amazing cavern and decked it out with all the amenities."

"It's terrific and a great memento of your father. What did he do for a living?"

"When I was young, he was a lumber-camp foreman when we lived in Pennsylvania. Dad was a strong, imposing figure and lumberjacks are a tough lot. Keeping them in line was no picnic, but he was able to command their respect. I don't remember a lot from those early days. We lived in a very small town of about two hundred called Forksville. When I was five, my mother died of a freakish accident when she had a tooth pulled. It started hemorrhaging and she bled to death. Shortly thereafter, my father moved the family to Wheaton, Illinois, which was a bustling metropolis compared to tiny Forksville. He had four brothers and a sister living there that could provide some family support, but before long he decided to send my two older sisters back to Pennsylvania to live with our grandparents. That just left my younger brother Garland and me. Money was extremely tight and Dad worked all the time doing odd jobs. Garland and I essentially raised ourselves; I did most of the household chores and cooking. My father eventually got a job as Wheaton's one-man police force."

"How about you? Any brothers or sisters?" he asks.

"No, it was just me. After I was born, my parents tried for a long time to have more kids, but it wasn't meant to be. It was lonely at times not having any other kids around and there wasn't anybody else to blame if something got broken but I managed to get by."

"How was it growing up in Los Angeles?" he asks.

"It was okay. For a lot of people, L.A. means Hollywood, sunshine, beaches and palm trees—a kind of fantasyland with movie stars and moguls, mansions with manicured lawns, tennis courts and swimming pools. That's not the Los Angeles I grew up in. Poverty, gangs and crime ruled my neighborhood. Row after row of small houses with bars on the doors and windows, front yards fenced with chain link and iron; buildings and back alleys tattooed with graffiti. People struggling to get by, nagged by the constant fear of random violence. Los Angeles—the Gang Capital of America.

"I grew up in a tiny house in Pacoima, tucked in the northeast part of the San Fernando Valley. The south and east portions of Los Angeles carry the reputation as the most notorious parts of the city, but the barrios in this corner of the Valley are every bit as dangerous when you're talking about gang violence, crime and drugs."

"It sounds like you were lucky to have made it out in one

piece," Red says. "Tell me about your parents."

"They met and married shortly after my father returned from serving in the Marine Corps. He saw combat duty during the Gulf War. They worked hard, doing the best they could with limited educations, scraping by to keep a roof over our heads. My mother worked at a hospital cleaning floors and emptying bed pans. Dad worked in construction. When I was growing up, he and I were inseparable. He coached me in football, basketball and baseball; he even taught me how to box.

"We *did* have a man cave however—our garage. It wasn't fancy—in fact it was pretty dingy—but it was our refuge and we spent much of our free time in there. Dad had it set up as a gym filled with an assortment of random weights he scavenged and second-hand boxing equipment. There was an old, faded poster of Muhammad Ali menacingly standing over a flattened Sonny Liston in the 1965 World Heavyweight title fight. USC football stuff was scattered around the walls. On a shelf next to the water heater, Dad had some photos and trophies from his days on the Marine Corps boxing team. Fighting is in our Irish blood and Dad loved the sweet science. He made sure I could defend myself by teaching me the fundamentals from a young age. We'd hit a worn-out heavy bag that was more duct tape than leather. To reach the speed bag, I'd have to stand on a folding chair. Every day he had a different regimen for me of pull-ups, push-ups and sit-ups mixed in with lifting weights, jumping rope and bag work. When I was about eight, he brought home some used gloves and headgear and he showed me and some of the kids in the neighborhood how to spar. The gloves were enormous and the headgear didn't fit very well, but we had a blast pounding away at each other.

"Ever since I can remember, my father admired USC and his plan was that I would go there on an athletic scholarship, hopefully football. He wanted me to have a better life. We lived in a dangerous place and he wanted me to get out when I was old enough. School and sports were the ticket out."

"It had to be really hard on them when you died so young."

"I'm sure it was very difficult for my mom; however, we lost my father when I was twelve."

"How did he die?"

"My father had demons he couldn't overcome. He never talked to me about it, but my mother said the war left some deep emotional wounds that wouldn't heal. He used to wake up screaming in the middle of the night from bad dreams. Every night he drank a lot, said he needed it to sleep. Mom and I were concerned about his drinking. I remember a time when I was about ten years old . . ."

The memories come rushing back and tumble out in words of pain and fear and anger.

It was late one night; I woke up and went into the kitchen. Dad's sitting at the table with his back to me. He lurches with surprise as I walk by.

"Geez Kyle, you 'bout scared me half to death. I'm going to

have to put a bell on you if you're going to be creeping around in the middle of the night."

"Sorry, Dad, I just needed to get a glass of water."

Rubbing his soggy face and bloodshot eyes, he slides his pistol off the table to hide it on his lap. He empties the last of a whiskey bottle into his glass and strains to focus on me.

"Dad, what's the gun out for?"

"Oh . . . uh . . . I thought I heard something outside and went to check it out but it was nothing."

Seeing him in this condition is nothing new, but the gun is a worrisome addition. "Are you okay?"

"I'm fine, son, I just couldn't sleep."

But the look on his face says otherwise. I wrap my arms around his neck and rest my head on his shoulder. He begins to choke up trying to hold back the tears, but they come anyway. Feeling my father's pain overwhelms me as I tighten my grasp and begin to cry.

"It's okay, son. Everything's gonna be all right. It's late; we need to get to bed."

Walking to my bedroom he puts a hand on my shoulder and uses the other to reach for anything along the way that might keep him from stumbling over. "I love you, Kyle," he says, tucking me into bed. He clicks off the bedroom light and I hear his staggering footsteps shuffle down the hallway.

About two years later, I'm walking home from school and unexpectedly see his truck in our driveway. That dreadful afternoon always haunts my memory. I walk in the front door and shout,

"Dad, I'm home!" I grab a juice box from the refrigerator and head to my bedroom; I'm buried with homework. Nearly an hour passes and I still haven't seen him. The house is unusually quiet. I figure he must be in the garage so I go out back to check. The garage door is closed so I go to the side door. I look in and my eyes freeze in disbelief. A chilling cold rushes over me and the blood draining from my head leaves me dizzy. I feel like I'm going to be sick. Dad is completely still, hanging from a beam with a strap around his neck. The folding chair I used to stand on is lying on its side below him. His bluish face is contorted in a gruesome expression that has a peculiar trace of peacefulness. I run to the house to call Mom at work, but only get a few feet outside as a blast of nausea brings me to my knees, throwing up until my stomach feels like it's been turned inside out . . .

Red's hushed voice gently draws me out of the darkness of the memory. "What a nightmare, Kyle, especially for a young kid. I'm truly sorry to hear that. How did you get along after his death?"

"It was the worst time of my life. After the shock wore off, I fell into a grim depression. I didn't feel like doing anything, not even getting out of bed in the morning. My mother and I were both devastated. She took a second job at night doing janitorial work in an office building to pay the bills. She said the constant work helped keep her mind off the pain and sorrow. We only saw each other briefly each night when she got home. I became a latchkey kid, started ditching school and getting into trouble.

I dropped out of sports and began hanging around with the wrong crowd. I was heartbroken to have lost my dad, but even more so, I was filled with anger. He was my hero; I idolized him and couldn't understand how he could take his own life and leave us. I've never been able to come to terms with it."

"I understand how you feel, Kyle. That was a terrible loss but carrying that kind of emotion around isn't healthy. It's impossible to truly understand what someone else is going through. Your father was human and we all make mistakes. I hope you're able to find a way to let those feelings go; try to remember your father for all the good he brought into your life."

"Thanks Red, I appreciate your advice. I've been trying to let go for a long time."

"With your dad gone and your mother working all the time, it had to have been pretty easy to fall into the gang life," Red says. "How did you manage to steer clear of that?"

"I was really close to heading down the wrong path for good until I started high school. The football coach at San Fernando remembered me and my father from Pop Warner and called me into his office the first day of school. He knew how much we loved USC and started telling me about the history of the program and how Charles White and Anthony Davis played there. I began to think about how awesome it would be to play on the same high school field as two of USC's greatest players. Coach Carson got me interested in sports again and talked me into coming out for the team. He knew I needed help and took me under his wing. He became my mentor, helped me refocus on my goal of playing for USC and supported me every step of the way. I also got back into baseball and basketball. Between school and year-round sports, there wasn't time for anything else. The gangbangers left me alone."

"You're lucky Coach Carson came along when he did," says Red.

Belvedere begins to clear off the dinner table and asks, "Would you gentlemen care for brandy and cigars over by the fire?"

"That's very tempting, Belvedere, but I think we'll have to take a raincheck. Kyle, I have something I'd like to show you and get your thoughts on it. Would you be interested in joining me?"

"Sure, that would be great. I don't know where you get your energy. Do you guys ever sleep?"

"So far I haven't found much need for it around here," says the Ghost.

"They always say you can rest when you're dead; that's obviously not true," I reply. "You're pretty spry for an eighty-seven-year-old, Red. I hope I've got your stamina when I'm your age."

"You just have to remember to drink your Ovaltine," he says.

"I don't know what that is, but okay. Let's go!"

Snap!

8

Training Camp

"Welcome to the college football branch of purgatory," Red says as we wander around a vacant, dilapidated training facility that looks like something out of the early Cold War era. A practice field of dead grass and parched dirt sits next to a weather-beaten concrete building that houses a decrepit locker room and antiquated meeting rooms. It makes me think of something Bear Bryant might have dreamed up as an upgrade to his infamous hell camp in Junction, Texas.

"What do you think of the place?" Red half-jokingly asks.

"Honestly, it's pretty underwhelming, to say the least. College football has its own piece of purgatory and this is it?"

"Yep, I know it's not much to look at. It's really a fixer-upper," he says.

"You can say that again. Whose idea was this?" I ask.

"Walter Camp came up with the notion of a purgatory training camp after he died in 1925. He couldn't leave the game behind, so he devised this place as a way to stay connected and help evolve and advance the sport for the future. He was a true pioneer and really loved the game. Heck, he practically invented it. The innovations he established over one hundred thirty years ago remain the foundation of the sport."

"As I recall, he devised rules like the system of downs and the line of scrimmage, instituted eleven-man teams, created the quarterback position and helped select the first All-America teams. What do you think Camp would say if he saw this place today?" I ask.

"I know he'd be pretty disappointed," Red admits.

"What happened?" I ask.

"Walter started the place from humble beginnings and grew the camp as the popularity of college football spread back on earth. Increasingly, the souls of former players and coaches came through and Walter worked with them personally to resolve whatever issues they might have had with the game. You see, as ghosts, we are not allowed to interfere with anything that happens on earth. Mortals have free will and must have the freedom to do as they choose. This camp was a way the spirit world could help evolve the game. When those footballers died, they would be directed to make a stop here and work with Walter before going on to heaven. Eventually, they would return to earth with new lives and elevate the game."

"How did he help them?" I ask.

"You name it, he did it. Walter mentored players who were habitual fumblers or dropped wide-open passes. He cured others who were prone to jumping offsides or making false starts. Camp had the patience to deal with boneheaded mistakes like committing dead ball fouls or running for touchdowns but letting go of the ball before crossing the goal line.

"Walter tutored coaches whose teams committed too many turnovers or penalties. He helped the ones that had trouble getting the right number of players on the field or got brain cramps making critical decisions with the game on the line.

"When John Heisman died in 1936, he was sent here to the training camp. Heisman was a legendary coach, but he had an unseemly practice of running up the score against severely undermanned opponents. His 1901 Clemson team beat Guilford College, 122–0, the most points ever scored in Clemson history. However, the topper came in 1916 when he coached Georgia Tech to an unmerciful beating of Cumberland College, 222–0. It was the most lopsided college football game ever played. Walter counseled Heisman about how to coach more responsibly and know when to take his foot off the gas.

"George Gipp was another," Red continues. "Gipp was stuck drifting around purgatory for years, unable to secure his passage through the Pearly Gates until Camp came along. The Gipper was one of the best players in Notre Dame history, but he was also a compulsive pool hustler, card shark, and gambler. As a student, Gipp was rarely seen around campus, but he could regularly be found in town at a pool hall or card game. Walter helped him resolve his gambling obsession and move on to the promised land.

"Others, like members of the powerhouse Army football program that were caught up in a massive academic cheating scandal in 1951, filtered through the camp over the years to atone for their misdeeds.

"Walter Camp built this place into a burgeoning institution that was making significant progress advancing college football. Unbeknownst to anyone on earth, his spirit has been impacting the game from beyond the grave since the first souls he started working with here began reincarnating on earth. In addition to producing better players and coaches, Walter's disciples inspired some of the game's most significant advancements like the wishbone offense, the integration of college football in the South, the adoption of overtime to settle ties, the two-point conversion, and the dawn of instant replay.

"But after forty years at the helm, it was time for Walter to move on. In 1965, when Amos Alonzo Stagg died, Walter tabbed him as the natural successor. Stagg, the Grand Old Man of Football, was ecstatic about his new opportunity. Shortly after he arrived, he created the facility you see here. Believe it or not, back then, it was considered state of the art. After a while though, his enthusiasm for the training camp began to wither.

"When Stagg was back on earth, he lived to be a hundred and two years old. He had coached football for sixty-eight years until he was forced to retire at the age of ninety-six. By the time he got here, he was flat-out dog-tired. When Woody Hayes showed up in 1987, he begged Stagg to help him with his anger issues, but Amos just didn't have anything left in the tank. He would spend most of his days rocking in a chair watching the grass grow and taking catnaps. Word spread; spirits weren't getting any help here. Over time, fewer and fewer college footballers came through. More and more souls were being ticketed straight through to heaven when they died. Gradually, the camp fell into total decline.

"By the time I kicked the bucket in 1991, the camp had become nothing more than an afterthought—a ghost town without any ghosts. Stagg was moved upstairs and the powers that be wanted me to take on a new position as the spiritual overseer of college football, a kind of ambassador for the game. I always wanted to give back and stay involved so I jumped at the chance. It's mainly a ceremonial post, but I love it. I spend my time watching over the game and enjoy every moment of it.

"When I took over, the angels filled me in about the camp's history and mentioned that if I would go about reviving it, they would be extremely grateful. That was twenty-eight years ago and I haven't done a thing with the place. I've been having the time of my afterlife, but I really haven't done anything to help the game. The longer I've been in purgatory, the more guilty I feel when I think about this camp, knowing the good it could bring if it was run properly. I'm just not a very good fit for the position. It requires organization, strategy and coaching; that's not me. I thought if you and I put our heads together we might be able to come up with some ideas to get the place going again. What do you say?"

My mind starts racing with the possibilities. "If we could turn this place around, I think it would be incredible!"

"I was hoping you'd say that. Where do you think we should begin?"

"For starters, I think we should expand the idea of the camp beyond just players and coaches. We should have a bigger picture and bring in others that are connected to the game."

"What do you have in mind?" he asks.

"Obviously, referees could use all the help they can get. What about college administrators? How about the fans? The game isn't worth much if not for the people who are committed to watching it."

"Wow, this place could get crowded," Red says.

"Think of the impact we can have on the game! We can enlist Jessica and her fellow angels to bring in all the help we need to staff the place. First thing we need to do is blow up this ancient relic of a facility and create a whole new camp."

I start designing a holographic scale model of the new training camp complete with lush green practice fields, a gleaming new headquarters building with locker rooms, weight rooms, meeting rooms and offices that rival anything Phil Knight could pay for.

"Players, coaches and trainers will have access to the most advanced training facilities and technology that we can dream up," I explain. "For the referees, we'll have rooms filled with TV monitors where they sit and watch non-stop footage of all the atrocious calls they've made, a sort of aversion therapy. It will have to be kept really cold in there, so they don't fall asleep. We'll call it Ice Station Zebra. Over here we'll have an Ivory Tower for the administrative types who've corrupted the game. We'll make them sit up there and think about what they've done to hurt the game until we feel they're ready to come out. For the fans, we can have an enormous sports bar with a round-the-clock party. Alcohol is the cause of most fan behavior problems so we'll go right to the source to deal with these issues."

Red is silent as he looks over the model. "What do you think? Do you like it?" I ask.

"I'm speechless. You just came up with all of this off the top of your head?"

"What can I say? I used to eat, sleep and live football. I literally don't have a life, so it comes kind of easy for me to think this stuff up."

"I knew I came to the right guy," he says. "This looks tremendous; I wouldn't change a thing."

I snap my fingers and, in a flash, we're standing in the middle of the brand-new training camp. "Welcome to Camp Grange—Home of the Galloping Ghost."

9

"In Heaven There Is No Beer"

The angels were ecstatic to see the new Camp Grange and immediately gave their seal of approval to our operation. They recruited and trained volunteer souls to help as counselors throughout the facility and began funneling the appropriate spirits here as they passed away on earth.

Looking out over the compound from our spacious offices in the penthouse of the headquarters, Red says, "You're doing a heck of a job here, Kyle; the camp is incredible. In fact, it's so nice we may have trouble getting our guests to leave once their time is up. Seriously, if people on earth knew about this place, they'd be dying to get in."

"Ugh," I groan sarcastically. "You've got to work on some new jokes. That one's as old as . . . "

"As old as I am?" he interrupts.

"Yeah, good point. Never mind. Listen, we've got to get to work. The angels gave me a list of mortals they've got their eyes on who will be coming here in the future. We need to review it so we know what to expect."

I walk over to the desk and pick up the bulky scroll. As I begin to read, the parchment unravels from my hands, spilling to the floor, unfurling a list that sprawls several feet across the carpet. Red and I look at each other in wide-eyed amazement.

"We're certainly going to have our hands full around here," he says with a laugh.

"Hmm, there are some familiar characters on the list," I notice. "A head coach who had to resign less than a week after landing a job at a top program because he falsified the credentials on his resumé. Another who lost his head coaching position at a premier program before he ever coached a game because of his reputation for being the life of too many sordid parties. There's the father who was seeking a six-figure payment from a school in exchange for enrolling his son to play quarterback there. Here's a coach that had been implicated in numerous infractions over his career but was finally undone by misrepresenting his knowledge of his players' improper relationships with a local tattoo parlor."

"That's a familiar lesson," Red says. "It's not the violation that does you in; it's the cover-up that gets you."

"That last coach is joined on the list by the fellow who was president of the school at that time," I add. "He's been designated for assignment here because, among other things, after the details of the coach's cover-up became public, the president was asked at a press conference if he ever considered firing the coach over this matter. He responded, 'No, are you kidding? Let me be very clear: I'm just hoping the coach doesn't dismiss me.'"

"He'll have plenty of time in the Ivory Tower to think about his missteps when he gets here," says Red.

As I continue down the list, I notice there aren't nearly as many future enrollees that are going to need help with Xs and Os type of stuff compared to those with issues involving academic fraud, corruption, drugs, alcohol and petty crime. "From the looks of things," I say, "we're going to be running more of a rehab center than a football training camp."

"At least we don't have to deal with the really bad apples," says Red. "Those reprobates are sent straight down to the inferno, never to be heard from again. The souls we're helping are generally headed in the opposite direction; they just need a little assist before they can reach the great beyond. Nobody's perfect, but we all have one thing in common: we're crazy about college football."

Finally, reaching the end of the lengthy scroll I notice a special disclaimer which reads, "Please Be Advised—There are countless players that have received improper cash benefits during their playing days that could be directed to your purgatory training camp for reformation upon their earthly demise. In fact, over the years, some college players were so well compensated they had to take a pay cut when they entered the NFL. However, since a satisfactory resolution to the issue of student-athlete compensation is so long overdue, it has been decided that, from this point forward, there will be no further spiritual sanctions imposed on these players regarding this issue."

"That's good to hear," says Red. "Players have been getting the short end of the stick for a long time."

"I agree. However, my biggest concern at the moment is our current enrollment." I pull up a spreadsheet that shows our camper head count by department. "The areas for players, coaches, referees and administrators are filling up quite slowly; on the other hand, the section for the fans at the sports bar is already reaching capacity."

"That makes sense," says Red. "There's a heck of a lot more fans out there than those directly involved in the game. We'll have to think about expanding the place or maybe try to move them up faster to Saint Peter."

"By the way," I recall, "Jessica told me the big boss has been distressed about the way fan behavior has been eroding over the years and he likes what we're doing with the sports bar. I've been doing some research and it's undeniable that most of the problems with fans involve alcohol. Too much of it and things can go bad in a hurry. But there's more to it than that. Psychologically, people have a built-in desire to belong to a group and that leads to what the shrinks call the ingroup and outgroup phenomenon. It's what fuels any rivalry. Basically, we love our team and we hate our rivals. You combine that with the pack mentality and good people can end up doing things they would never ordinarily do on their own. In certain circumstances, people instinctively feel that they can get away with bad behavior as an anonymous member of a group. It's one of the ways riots get started and grow out of control.

"Also, I learned that hormones can play a role in bad behavior.

Research has shown that men can get a big surge of testosterone just by watching their team win. They can even get as much of a jolt as the players themselves and that rush can lead to aggressive behavior. Add excessive amounts of alcohol to all these factors and it's no wonder fans can do crazy things. I've had the counselors set up a few interviews for us with some of the campers. Let's head over there and check in on the operation."

• • •

Red's Gridiron is the largest sports bar you've ever seen. It's easily the size of a football field with several massive bars, huge TVs everywhere, and the distinct smell of chicken wings and stale beer lingering in the air. It's packed with souls wearing every imaginable form of fan attire representing every school you can think of and many more you've never heard of. They're playing darts, pinball, foosball, air hockey, Pop-A-Shot, Pac-Man, video golf and pool. The booze flows like water and everyone seems to be having a great time. We have bouncers conspicuously scattered around the place keeping a constant watch over things. You've got to keep your eyes open in a place like this. Every now and then, a fight can break out or an occasional bottle will get thrown. If we do have any trouble, the bouncers are right on top of it to maintain order.

Moving through the crowd, we see a guy sporting a bright orange-and-blue mullet with his school's logo shaved into the side of his head. He's standing on a chair guzzling a pitcher of beer while his friends cheer him on.

"Go! Go! Go! Go!" they chant.

He's spilling as much as he's drinking, but he still gets a roar from the group when he proudly raises the empty pitcher over his head and yells in triumph.

Everywhere you look, there are fans with their faces and bodies painted to show their school spirit. Mohawks, faux hawks and fright wigs in every color of the rainbow dot the landscape of this crazy party. There are Green Men doing bizarre dance moves around the bar. An overweight, shirtless guy is standing up waving a jersey over his head yelling at people to get up and cheer for his team. We pass by a group of despondent fans, frozen in disbelief, watching their school lose a big game while another group, with paper bags over their heads, watches as their team extends its record-breaking losing streak. A guy with his hands full of beers takes an accidental blindside hit from another fan and beer goes flying everywhere. Tempers flare immediately, but cooler heads prevail as the bouncers defuse the calamity and the mop and bucket crew cleans up the mess. It might have been a different story if we charged for drinks here, but everything is always on the house. We grab a seat in a quiet booth in a far corner of the bar and one of the waitresses comes by.

"Hi Katie," says Red. "How's everything going?"

"Business as usual," she says. "Everybody's been behaving

themselves. What can I get you fellas?"

"How about an order of those delicious bacon cheddar jalapeno poppers and a couple of beers?" he replies.

"Comin' right up."

The waitresses, bartenders and bouncers are all trained camp counselors—volunteer souls brought in by the angels to help run the bar. They could all be in heaven if they wanted to, but they choose to help us out here. It's kind of a personal mission for each of them, earning points in heaven. They can leave whenever they want, but few ever go.

All the campers here have made some type of blunder as a fan that has kept them out of heaven. The transgressions they've committed on earth are not bad enough to warrant them spending the rest of eternity in perdition, but until they're absolved of their mistakes, they're stuck here. Most of what we get are fans who had too much to drink and did something stupid.

Different from other parts of the camp, the wrinkle we have here in Red's Gridiron is that all the campers think they've died and gone to heaven. They all buy into it when they first arrive—a non-stop party in the ultimate sports bar where you can watch football, eat and drink as much as you want, and play games forever. On the surface, it looks like a dream come true for a fan; however, most start to gradually figure out this isn't the ultimate reward and realize they need to learn how to move on.

The bartenders and waitresses do the heavy lifting determining which ones have recognized this probably isn't heaven and are ready to admit their mistakes and pledge their remorse. Red and I do the final interviews and if everything checks out, we send them upstairs to Saint Peter.

Katie comes back with our beers and poppers and asks if we're ready to get started.

"Bring 'em on," I say, raising my beer to Red. "Here's mud in your eye, pal."

A waitress escorts a young fellow over to the booth and introduces him. "Gentlemen, this is Tom," she says. "He looks forward to speaking with you."

"Hello Tom, have a seat. My name is Harold and this is my good friend Kyle."

After some small talk, Tom explains that he's been here a couple of weeks and has had a great time, but he's been getting restless and feels there's something not quite right here.

"The free booze, food, games and non-stop party is a lot of fun, but there has to be more to heaven than this," he says. "I started talking to one of the bartenders and he suggested I think back to see if there is anything in my past that might be bothering me. Before long, I recalled an incident and went back to talk to him about it. He said there was someone he wanted me to meet so here I am."

"We're glad you're here Tom," I say. "Tell us what's on your mind."

"Back when I was in college, our team won a big game against our archrival. There had been a lot of pent-up frustrations among everyone connected with the university because it had been so long since we last beat them. When the game ended, all of us in the student section poured out onto the field to celebrate. A few minutes later, the huge mob headed toward the goalposts. Several of us climbed onto the crossbar to bring it down but it wouldn't budge. More people climbed on; still nothing. Finally, it snapped loose and crashed to the ground. It's remarkable no one got hurt. We broke the posts off the crossbar and started to parade them around the field. We headed toward our cheering section and everyone was screaming and celebrating. We decided to toss one of the posts into the stands as a souvenir for the fans and that's when several people got hurt. Luckily, nothing serious, mainly just some bumps and bruises, but it definitely took some of the fun out of it. A couple of days later I read a story about a girl who had been hit in the head a few years earlier by a goalpost as it was being torn down and she was almost killed. It crushed her skull and she suffered a serious brain injury. She managed to survive, but her life was never the same as she struggled to overcome paralysis in her legs and arms. I've always regretted what we did that night. It was a ridiculous and dangerous thing to do, but I had been drinking and got caught up in the excitement."

"Thanks for telling us your story," I say. "We can appreciate your regrets. That's good enough for me," I say, glancing over at Red.

He gives me an acknowledging nod and turns to Tom. "Son, you'll be happy to know your instincts were right about this place. It's not heaven, but kind of a proving ground to figure things out before you make the final step and we believe you passed. We're recommending that you go see a good friend of ours and, we're confident that when you tell him your story, he'll welcome you into heaven with open arms. It was a pleasure meeting you and best of luck. By the way, be sure to bring along a good book; I heard the line to get in up there is really long."

I motion for the waitress to come over and say, "This gentleman is good to go. Could you please direct him upstairs to Saint Peter and send over the next candidate?"

A woman, who looks to be in her early fifties, sits down and introduces herself. She proceeds to tell us about an episode in her college days when she was at a football game and was discovered passed out on the floor of the women's restroom. She had been at a tailgate party that started early that morning and had been drinking all day long and hadn't had much to eat. By the time the game started late that afternoon, she was a goner. She staggered into the game with the help of some friends and made it to her seat where she promptly fell asleep. She remembers waking up during the game feeling sick and rushed to the restroom. She said she made it inside before she blacked out. The next thing she remembered is waking up in the emergency room several hours later. She had severe alcohol poisoning. One of her friends came in to see her and explained that when she didn't return to her seat, she became concerned and went to look for her. She found her lying face down in a pool of vomit on the floor of the restroom. It was not a pretty sight. She was still breathing so her friend ran to get help. The paramedics took her to the emergency room where they pumped her stomach and got her cleaned up. She said it was one of the scariest, most embarrassing times in her life and she regretted it deeply. Red thanks her for coming to see us and we pass her on upstairs.

"Those late afternoon and night games can be a real problem," Red says. "Lots of fans start tailgating early in the morning and end up drinking all day long. By the time the game rolls around, many of them are three sheets to the wind. Stadium security always has many more problems at night games with drunken behavior and fighting as opposed to day games. There's just more time for people to drink too much before the game starts. Regardless of the alcohol problem, I've always believed that football should be played on Saturdays in the middle of the day. Sadly, that isn't possible anymore due to television, which dictates all the starting times to fit their schedule."

A few minutes later, another fellow sits down and tells us his tale about the time he thought it would be a good idea to run out on the field during a game. He was having fun running around for a few moments as he avoided being tackled by a portly security guard. However, the fun stopped when the police joined the pursuit and tasered him, which immediately dropped him to the ground. He said the pain was excruciating. After they shut off the electricity, they zip-tied his hands behind his back and escorted him off the field. He spent the night in jail, was fined over $1,000 and was banned from the stadium.

Other stories include a woman who had a bit too much to drink and flashed the jumbotron in the stadium. People started cheering her on and she continued to lift her top. She finally took it off and started to swing it around over her head. The crowd lifted her up and surfed her to the top of the stadium. She lost her shirt in the process and had to walk topless back down to her seat until security escorted her away.

Another fellow tells us about how he smuggled some road flares into a stadium. He was upset at a call during the game, ignited one of the flares, and threw it onto the field. It hit a referee on the head and knocked his cap off. Luckily, he wasn't hurt.

The last person we talk to tells us that he went to a game where his seats were in the first row of the upper deck of a stadium. He had been drinking and started walking down the aisle to his seat. There was a hand railing running down the center of the aisle, so he sat on it and began to slide down. As he got to the bottom he couldn't stop and fell over the railing. He dropped about twenty-five feet and landed on another fan, who sustained neck and shoulder injuries. Amazingly, the guy that fell two and a half stories ended up virtually unharmed.

That wraps up our interviews; everyone we talked to was genuinely repentant for what they did, and we feel that they had learned from their mistakes. In total we send all six of them up to Saint Peter. A waitress comes over and tells us that in the time we spent doing the interviews, they had received over twenty new arrivals.

"We're going to need a bigger bar," says Red.

10

Breakthrough

"At the rate new fan arrivals are coming into the Gridiron," I mention to Red, "I think we should expand the place and start delegating more of our responsibilities to some of the senior staff in order to speed up the process. Jessica said they like the results we're producing upstairs so they're going to be sending even more our way. It's just too much for you and me to manage that kind of volume."

"I'm with you on that," he says. "They've really got us hopping around here and we've got our hands full keeping up with the new marching orders they've given us."

Shortly after we opened the camp for business, Jessica, who's become our main emissary with the powers that be upstairs, explained that another area they'd like us to give special attention to is the medical and training department to focus on ways to reduce chronic football injuries. We've been getting former players coming through who have dealt with serious injuries throughout their careers, and our staff has been doing research on ways to reduce and prevent them whenever possible.

"I'm excited about the possibilities of how we might be able to have an impact on making the game safer," I say. "I was lucky when I played, at least until my heart gave out. Aside from the usual aches and pains, I played eight years of organized football and never had a serious injury. The worst thing that ever happened was at the end of my senior season of basketball. I went up for a dunk on a fast break and got low-bridged by an opposing player. I took an awkward fall backwards and broke my throwing arm, which wiped out my senior year of baseball. I was going to play baseball as my backup plan in case football didn't work out. It was pretty disappointing at the time because, prior to the injury, I was projected as a potential first round draft pick as a pitcher. Despite missing the season, the Pittsburgh Pirates were still interested and drafted me in the third round, but I already had my scholarship to SC and was committed to playing football."

"Too bad even your backup plan didn't work out," says the Ghost. "I know you would have had a great pro career whichever sport you played.

"Between high school, college, and the pros, I played organized football for eighteen years. I was always playing hurt with cuts, bruises, bites, broken noses and concussions. When I was a young boy, I played sandlot games against the older kids and usually paid the price by getting hurt. Once I got kicked in the back and couldn't sit down for two weeks. I'd often get cuts around my eyes and would need to get them stitched up. I wanted to stop playing football when I was younger, but my dad always encouraged me to keep playing. He used to tell me, 'Life is tough. Football helps you tackle your fears and prepares you to face an uncertain future and become a man.' I never forgot that.

"In four years of high school football, I was only seriously injured once. I got kicked in the head during a game my senior year and was knocked unconscious. I didn't wake up for almost two full days. When I finally came to, I had trouble talking for the next few days.

"In my sophomore year at Illinois, I took a shot to the chest against Nebraska that was so hard I thought I'd broken my back. I continued playing even though it felt like the splintered ends of my broken ribs were scraping against my lungs. However, one of the most painful injuries I ever experienced was when I dislocated my shoulder and they had to pop it back into the socket. Ugh, that really hurt. I recovered from each of those injuries without any lingering effects, but in 1927 I suffered an injury that put an end to my glory days as the Galloping Ghost."

"That was the knee injury in your third year in the pros, right?" I say. "I saw that up close in the newsreel Jessica put me through. That was painful to watch. Your knee twisted and then broke loose sideways. I'll never forget the sound; it was kind of like . . . "

"Stop! Enough! It hurts to even think about it," he says. "My knee was never the same after that. I couldn't cut and change pace, which is what had made me such a threat in the open field. It was so unstable I couldn't put any lateral pressure on my knee or it would give out. I made the mistake of coming back a few weeks after the injury and played several games through the end of the season in tremendous pain. I was twenty-four and believed I could play myself back into shape, but in the end, I did irreparable damage to the knee. I thought my career was finished; as a football player, your legs are your greatest asset. I was out of football for over a year. Eventually, I was able to run again and regained a lot of my speed, but it was all straight ahead. Luckily, it allowed me to make a comeback and I was able to play another six years.

"As tough as the game is today, it's nothing compared to how dangerous it was back in the early days in terms of violence and death," he says. "Before the forward pass was adopted in 1905, football was a bruising ground game that relied mainly on brute force to advance the ball downfield. Nobody had any protective equipment and offenses used mass formations like the flying wedge, where helmetless players locked arms and became human battering rams slamming into similarly aligned defenses. Crushed skulls, ruptured organs and broken bones were commonplace."

"I read that Harvard banned football from its campus for eleven years in 1860 because it was too violent," I say. "Their rivalry game against Yale in 1894 was so brutal it was called the 'Hampden Park Blood Bath' because there were so many serious injuries. Army and Navy canceled their annual rivalry game for five years beginning in 1894 because their games were so violent, and schools like Georgia and Georgia Tech suspended their football programs altogether. The game was so dangerous that between 1890 and 1905, it was estimated that three hundred and thirty college football players died from injuries playing football. In 1905 alone, there were nineteen reported deaths."

"That's when Teddy Roosevelt got involved," says Red. "The president was a big fan of the game and had sons that played football, but there was a huge public outcry about the fatalities. He got representatives from Princeton, Yale and Harvard together that year to reform the sport."

"The following year," I add, "they formed the Intercollegiate Football Rules Committee which later became the NCAA. Walter Camp was part of that group that instituted new rules to make the game safer. Legalizing the forward pass took away some of the trench warfare brutality and brought more speed, skill and agility to the game, making a significant impact on lessening the fatalities and major injuries.

"Speaking of which, we should head over to the training department and check in with Russ Johnston to see what kind of progress they're making."

Russell Johnston oversees our training staff and works with the doctors and scientists in our research labs. We were fortunate that Jessica was able to recruit him to come work with us. Back in his days on earth, Russ was involved in athletic training for over forty years, working with collegiate and Olympic athletes, developing advanced physical conditioning programs and pioneering the treatment of sports injuries, while caring for over 40,000 athletes.

"Russ, it's good to see you," I say. "What's the latest on the injury front from the training department?"

"As you can imagine, some of the most common types of injuries that we're seeing in today's game are sprains, fractures, dislocations, and concussions," he says. "When they finally outlawed spearing in 1976, that led to a significant drop in major injuries. Today, catastrophic injuries to the spine are uncommon and fatalities in football are rare. The knee remains the most common point of injury for college football players and accounts for about seventeen percent of all injuries."

"I can relate to that," says the Ghost. "Mine almost ended my career."

"As common as knee injuries are," Russ replies, "advancements in surgical techniques have made successful recoveries an everyday occurrence. Torn ACLs and other ligament and joint damage no longer represent the potential career enders they used to back in the day. However, players continue to get bigger, stronger and faster which leads to more powerful collisions, both with other players and impacts with the ground. Also, their increased size and speed contribute to more non-contact knee injuries from cutting and change of direction, especially on artificial turf."

"What are you seeing as far as improvements to equipment?" I ask.

"Helmets and pads are a double-edged sword because they provide necessary protection but also increase the violence of the game," Russ replies. "Until recently, football helmets had remained unchanged since the 1970s—a hard-plastic shell with foam padding inside."

"I played in the leatherhead era," says Red, "and helmets weren't even required to be worn back then. It wasn't until 1939 that they became mandatory equipment."

"New technology is improving the protection provided by some of today's state-of-the-art helmets," says Russ. "Research is being done to design helmets for specific position groups to provide better protection, because players experience different types of impacts depending on the position they play. We always emphasize that the helmet should be used for protection and not as a weapon.

"Teams are also embracing improved blocking and tackling techniques that take the head out of the play. Rugby style tackling that initiates contact with the shoulders or chest can reduce injuries and be a more effective technique to get players to the ground. Players should always try to keep their head up when tackling and running with the ball."

"That's a challenge because you instinctively want to lower your head and shoulders when you approach contact," says Red. "The guy with the lower pad level usually wins."

"I agree. I didn't say change was going to be easy," he replies, "but the game needs to continue to evolve to make it safer.

"In terms of fatalities," he continues, "factors leading to overexertion have been the leading cause of death in football since the beginning of the twenty-first century. Years ago, college training camps were brutal endeavors with two-a-day practices in full pads and continuous hitting."

"Kyle, that reminds me of Bear Bryant's hell camp in Texas you mentioned earlier," says Red. "Talk about overexertion. Russ, do you remember hearing about that?"

"Vaguely; refresh my memory," he says.

"Bryant had just taken over at Texas A&M in 1954," I say. "He was determined to turn their program around and that first training camp was intended to toughen up his players and get rid of the quitters; it worked. Bryant bussed the team nearly three hundred miles away from campus to a crude outpost in Junction, Texas, that was mostly dirt, weeds, rocks, and rattlesnakes. They arrived in two Greyhound buses; ten days later, they returned home in one. The camp was held during severe drought conditions and an intense heat wave where temperatures typically rose above one hundred degrees. Bryant held four-hour practice sessions and didn't allow any water breaks. Exhausted players were routinely dragged off the field by their heels. There was no qualified training or medical staff on hand. It was a miracle that no one died. Each day, players quit in droves; many just ran off in the middle of the night. They estimated that ninety players started the camp and only thirty-five remained at the end."

"Those types of practices were thought to toughen players up," Russ says. "In hindsight, they were extremely dangerous. If anyone tried running a camp like that today they'd be thrown in jail.

"All that aside," he says, "the most significant injury issue facing the game today is brain trauma, most commonly due to concussions. Concussions are thought to represent about seven percent of all college football injuries."

"I can't begin to tell you how many concussions I had throughout my career," says Red. "During my first year as a pro, I think I had at least ten concussions. One game I got knocked unconscious in the second quarter. Later, I came to and went back into the game in the fourth quarter and scored the game's only touchdown. I'm surprised I remember any of it."

"All that brain trauma most likely accounts for your Parkinson's disease toward the end of your life," says Russ.

"You're probably right," says Red, "although I consider myself lucky. I lived a long life in overall good health. Without a doubt football took its toll on me, but if given the choice I'd do it all over again."

"You're very fortunate," says Russ. "Concussions are a common type of injury that can happen in any sport. Most occur without the player being knocked unconscious and involve a short-term loss of brain function.

"If you guys remember back to your college anatomy class, the brain is an organ that is suspended in fluid inside the hard shell of the skull. Impacts to the head cause the brain to bounce back and forth or twist inside the skull, which can result in injury. That trauma creates chemical changes in the brain and can also sometimes stretch and damage brain cells. The effects of a concussion are usually temporary and most people fully recover from them.

"A common-sense approach is needed to prevent and manage head injuries. When a player sustains a head injury, they should receive immediate medical attention and shouldn't be allowed to return to play until given permission from a physician. Coaches should never make those decisions. A player with a brain injury needs sufficient time to heal and recover. Each player and each concussion is unique, and there is no set time frame for when they should return to the field."

"It makes sense that coming back too soon and then sustaining additional brain injuries can lead to more serious long-term problems," I say. "As players, we all want to play, but nowadays you need to be honest about reporting concussion symptoms."

"Absolutely!" says Russ. "It is believed that for every concussion that is identified, many more go unreported. Everyone involved with the game needs to be informed about concussions and brain injury and how to take the proper steps to prevent, identify and manage that part of the game.

"In the 1920s, researchers identified a condition in boxers called 'dementia pugilistica' or 'punch-drunk syndrome' which was likely caused by repetitive brain injury. That condition is now known as chronic traumatic encephalopathy or CTE and is believed to be related to brain injuries suffered in contact sports like football, soccer, hockey and rugby. CTE is a degenerative disease of the brain in which symptoms typically do not appear until years or even decades after an athlete has retired from the sport. There is no known cure for CTE, and diagnosis can only be made after a person's death by analyzing their brain. CTE has been diagnosed in the brains of former college and pro football players. Researchers back on earth are in the very early stages of understanding the disease. Not everyone who experiences repeated concussions goes on to develop CTE. Some people get it and others don't. It could take researchers years and even decades to fully grasp the cause and effect of CTE. Right now, there is a tremendous need for early detection of CTE while the person is still alive.

"With that in mind, Jessica and I have assembled an elite team of neurologists and scientists to address this issue. She has enlisted the spirit of Jean-Martin Charcot, who is regarded as the father of modern neurology, along with James Parkinson and Alois Alzheimer, all of them brilliant physicians, to lead our research effort into CTE. They have been working diligently alongside a staff of dedicated scientists who will not stop until they solve the puzzle of this troubling disease."

"That's great news, Russ," I say. "We can't thank you enough for taking the initiative to tackle this predicament. We really appreciate your help."

Just then, one of Russ' assistants enters the room and hands him a message. Russ gives it a quick glance. "Sorry for the interruption, gents. It's a note from Dr. Charcot; he'd like me to come to the lab as soon as possible—sounds important. Would you fellas like to join me?"

"By all means," says Red. "It would be a privilege to meet the group and see their operation."

As we walk down the corridor approaching the research lab, the sound of voices gets progressively louder.

"Sounds like a pretty enthusiastic group in there," I say. Russ gives me a quizzical look and shrugs his shoulders. He opens the door and we enter to a celebratory outburst.

"Gentlemen, welcome!" says a distinguished-looking man with a heavy French accent. "You've come at a wonderful time. Please join us for some champagne."

"Dr. Charcot, I presume," I say, reaching out my hand. "My name is Kyle McGinnis and this is my good friend Harold Grange."

"What a nice surprise," he replies. "It's a pleasure to meet you both." He turns to Red. "Ahhh, the famous Mr. Grange—The Galloping Ghost. It is an honor to have you here."

Russ makes the introductions among the rest of the group and then says, "Doctor, please share your good news. What are we celebrating?"

"Gentlemen, we have arrived at a breakthrough in our research into chronic traumatic encephalopathy," says Dr.

Charcot. "I will let Dr. Parkinson give you some of the background on the discovery."

"Thank you, Dr. Charcot," says Dr. Parkinson. "It has been determined that an abnormal buildup of a naturally occurring protein in the human brain called *tau* is the culprit behind CTE. This disease is characterized by abnormal changes in a person's behavior, mood, cognition and motor skills, often showing signs of depression, aggression and confusion. However, the disease cannot be diagnosed until examining the subject's brain after death. The irregular accumulation of tau protein becomes toxic and destroys healthy brain tissue. It has been described as the equivalent of pouring concrete down plumbing pipes. The vital first step in the treatment of CTE is early diagnosis.

"We have created research subjects in our laboratory that fully replicate living human beings with varying degrees of CTE. By employing a specialized radioactive compound that we developed, along with the use of positron emission tomography or PET scans, we are now able to clearly identify the irregular accumulation of tau protein associated with CTE in living subjects.

"That's fantastic news, doctor!" says Russ. "How does it work?"

"The radioactive tracer is injected into the bloodstream and attaches itself to the tau clusters," he says. "The PET scan picks up their radioactive glow, illuminating their exact location inside the brain, which is marked by a distinctive pattern that is unique to CTE.

"However, the most significant challenge we face in our work here is that our research process is the polar opposite of how we would go about it as humans on earth. In our spirit world, we are limited only by the boundaries of our own imaginations and we know we can create the solution to a problem simply by thinking it into existence. In this case, we knew we wanted a radioactive compound that would selectively attach itself to accumulations of tau protein in the brain. With the solution clearly defined, we were able to immediately bring the compound into being. From there, the real work began as we needed to deconstruct it to understand how it exists. Next, we had to ensure that it was something that could be re-created back on earth within the real-world boundaries of human existence. Our compound checks all these boxes."

"All this technical stuff is starting to make my head hurt," says Red.

Dr. Alzheimer jumps in. "As significant as this early detection is, there's more. We have been working on a new process of dynamic protein degradation that is designed to target and break down the tau accumulations in the brain and are confident that this advancement will be effective in reversing the effects of CTE and lead to a cure."

"This is beyond amazing news, gentlemen," I say. "You're all to be congratulated on your incredible work."

As I'm hearing about these fantastic developments, I'm nagged by a discouraging realization. Now that they've made these groundbreaking discoveries, it will still take years for them to reach earth.

"I wish there was a way we could get these discoveries down to earth immediately rather than waiting on reincarnation," I say. "All the work we do here is a long-term play. It takes years for a reincarnated spirit to grow up on earth and reach an age where they can put into effect the things they learn here."

"I'm afraid there's not much we can do about that, pal," says Red. "Rules are rules and it's out of our hands at this point."

"Gentlemen, there is no time to waste," says Dr. Charcot. "Once we finalize the cure, I will personally volunteer upstairs for reincarnation to hasten the process. Who knows, maybe I will come back to earth and deliver these discoveries as a boy genius."

"That's a monumental commitment, Doctor," says Red. "You were granted an eternity in heaven. Are you sure you want to go back to earth and do it again?"

"I am sure. After all, what good is a scientist if we can't put our work to use helping mankind."

"I will join you, Doctor," says Dr. Alzheimer, stepping forward. "I relish the opportunity to continue our work back on earth."

"Count me in as well," says Dr. Parkinson.

The room falls silent for a moment as the realization of these brilliant scientists' dedication sets in among the group.

"I propose a toast," says Dr. Charcot as champagne is

poured for everyone. "I am awe-struck by the devotion of my colleagues and humbled by the opportunity to carry on with you both in another lifetime. It is an honor to work with you. Godspeed to us all. À votre santé!"

"Cheers!" says the group.

11

Just Plain Hate

We leave the doctors to continue their work. Based on the discoveries they've made here, their contributions to the game should be historic, although it's frustrating that it takes so long for our work to make an impact on earth. However, working with Red to revitalize the training camp and be a part of what we've already accomplished has been tremendous.

"I feel like I'm getting a second chance here," I say to Red.

"What do you mean?" he asks.

"After I couldn't play football anymore, I really struggled to find a new direction in life. I loved the game so much and poured everything I had into it. When that dream was taken away, it was crushing—I felt cheated. I became a diehard fan and soaked up everything I could about the game, but it was a far cry from being able to play. I searched for a long time but was never able to find anything else that I really cared about—something that gave me a real purpose. I was lost—just going through the motions.

"But now, meeting you, getting the camp going and the things we're doing has been great. We're giving back to the game and we'll be making a real difference. I haven't been this excited about anything since I was playing. It feels like I'm being given another opportunity to make up for what I lost on earth."

"You deserve it," says Red. "You had some tough breaks in your life: losing your father to suicide, losing football and losing your life as a young man. It's difficult to understand how you ended up in purgatory. You'd think you would have gone straight to heaven after what you've been through. Whatever the reason, I'm glad you're here. I definitely needed help getting the camp off the ground and it's been pretty lonely haunting college football all these years by myself. It's just been me and Belvedere and he's not much of a football guy. It's terrific to have a pal around who loves it as much as I do.

"Speaking of Belvedere," he says, "we've been so wrapped up here, I feel like we've abandoned our old friend back at the Grotto. We should go check in and see how he's getting along. I know he feels a little neglected if we're gone too long. Also, it's rivalry week in college football. I always make it a point to get down to earth and check out one of the big games. Are you with me?"

"That sounds great," I say. "I could use a little break."

Snap!

• • •

The Grotto is dark and cold when we arrive.

"This is strange," says Red. "Belvedere always has the fire going and the lights on. Oh Belvedere!" he calls out.

We stand in the darkness for a moment waiting to see our old friend, but there's no response. Red snaps his fingers and the Grotto comes back to life. The fireplace crackles with a burst of flames and the oil lamps around the cave flicker on.

"Oh Belvedere!" he tries again. "I wonder where he could be. Belvedere's always here at a moment's notice."

Finally, the faithful servant appears. "I'm sorry, Mr. Red, were you waiting long?"

"No, old friend. It's good to see you. We've been away far too long. How have you been?"

"Fine sir, thank you," he replies with a forlorn sigh. "It's been quite a while since you gentlemen have been by, so I shut the place down and went to visit some of my old haunts down on earth."

"Taking a stroll down memory lane, huh?" Red asks. "I apologize for not checking in with you sooner. Kyle and I have been going non-stop at the training camp. You wouldn't believe the progress we've been making."

"That's wonderful news, sir. Can I bring you gentlemen anything?"

"No, I'm fine," says Red.

"I'm good, Belvedere," I say. "Why don't you have a seat and tell us about your visit?"

"Thank you, sir," he says. "I went down home to Savannah to wander around town. I stopped in at my favorite old pub where some of the other butlers from around town used to get together. The place hasn't changed much, but you don't see many traditional servant types around anymore. I went out to the home I used to work at. It's a grand old mansion filled with wonderful memories. The same family owned that place for generations, and I worked there nearly my entire life. They have moved on, but the current owners have taken great care to keep it in excellent condition. I wanted to see the place one last time."

"You don't expect to be getting down there again?" Red asks.

Belvedere pauses for a moment. "With all due respect, sir, I've been thinking about retiring. I've been working a long time and you don't seem to have much need for me around here any longer. I thought it might be time to go on to heaven."

Red is clearly saddened to hear his old friend might be leaving. "Belvedere, you've been such a great help to me for so many years," he says. "I owe you an eternal debt of gratitude. I would hate to see you go; are you sure this is what you want?"

"I really just want to be useful and feel like I'm being of service," he says, "but that doesn't seem to be the case here now."

"I have an idea!" I say. "Why don't you come work with us at the training camp? There's always something to do there; you'd be a tremendous help."

"That's a great idea, Kyle," says Red. "What do you say, Belvedere?"

"I don't know, sir. I'm not much of a football man."

"That's okay, you don't have to be," says Red. "You can help us however you'd like. You may even find some new things you enjoy doing as well. You're a valued member of the team, Belvedere, and we'd love to have you join us; at least give it a try."

"It would be good to feel useful again," he says. "I suppose there's no harm in taking a crack at it."

"That's the spirit old boy!" says Red. "You're gonna have a great time."

"In fact, Kyle and I were thinking about taking in a football game. Would you like to join us?"

"Hmm, it's not my cup of tea, sir. I don't really follow sports; I'd feel pretty out of place."

"This would be a great chance to learn," says Red. "You know, jump in with both feet. Plus, it's rivalry week down there—always some great games."

"Wouldn't know anything about it, sir," he replies. "My life as a butler has always kept me pretty isolated."

"Rivalry games are always some of the most exciting games in every sport, especially in college football," I say.

"How do these things get started?" he asks.

"When you have two schools that are reasonably close in size and geography and they play each other in a competitive matchup over a long period of time, it's usually the formula for a great rivalry. No matter how well or poorly each team is doing in any given year, you can usually throw out their records when they meet because anything can happen."

"When you play another school year after year, that familiarity breeds contempt and rivalries can evolve into vicious blood feuds," says Red. "Although, rival schools generally have a certain amount of respect and admiration for each other, even if they don't like to admit it."

"Do you know which two schools have played each other more often than any other rivalry in college football history?" I ask Red.

"It has to be a couple of the Ivy League schools," Red says. "Maybe Yale vs. Princeton or Harvard vs. Yale."

"You're close. Yale and Princeton are second, having played one hundred forty-two times starting in 1873. Harvard and Yale have played each other one hundred thirty-six times beginning in 1875 and the rivalry is the third longest running of all time. Do you give up?"

"Yep, I'm no match for your photographic memory," Red says.

"Lehigh University and Lafayette College," I answer.

"Ugh, you got me there," he says. "I always forget about that one."

"They've played each other one hundred fifty-five times starting in 1884," I say. "Those schools are only about seventeen miles from each other in Eastern Pennsylvania and in all those years, they only missed playing each other one time, and that was over one hundred years ago, in 1896."

"One of the things I really like about college rivalries are the terrific names they come up with," says Red. "Like the Backyard Brawl between Pittsburgh and West Virginia or the Red River Showdown between Texas and Oklahoma. They used to call that one the Red River Shootout but decided to change it because they didn't want to be seen as promoting gun violence."

"How about the Border War between Kansas and Missouri," I add. "BYU and Utah even bring religion into it with their annual Holy War.

"One of the most colorful names in the country for a college football rivalry is something that the two schools actually want to get rid of but can't seem to shake. The World's Largest Outdoor Cocktail Party between Georgia and Florida can draw over a half million people down to Jacksonville. In the past, the partying has gotten so over the top that the schools and the city have tried for years to change the name; however, nobody's buying in. Changing that name is like trying to stuff a genie back in the bottle.

"When you're talking about names, schools can despise each other so much that *hate* becomes the most accurate description. Some even put it right in the name, like Western Kentucky and Middle Tennessee calling their matchup One Hundred Miles of Hate or Georgia and Georgia Tech with Clean, Old-Fashioned Hate.

"Many of the games are bitterly fought over perpetual trophies which are often items of little monetary value but have become priceless treasures because of their history. For example, one of the oldest and most famous trophies for a rivalry game is the Little Brown Jug, which is given to the winner of the Michigan versus Minnesota game. Do you know the story behind that trophy?"

"No, but I have a feeling you're going to tell us," says Red.

"You're right! Back in 1903, Michigan traveled to play at Minnesota, and the Wolverine coach, Fielding Yost, was worried that Minnesota might try to contaminate their water supply for the game. He asked a student manager to go buy a five-gallon jug so they could carry their own water. After a tough game that ended in a 6–6 tie, Michigan forgot the jug on the bench and returned home. When they realized their oversight and asked for it to be returned, the Gophers decided that if Michigan wanted it back, they would have to play for it. It took a few years, but the teams finally met again, and that thirty-cent clay jug became a prized trophy the two schools would fight over for the next hundred years."

"Being an Illinois alum," says Red, "I know that trophy games are very popular, especially in the Big Ten. Purdue and Indiana play for the Old Oaken Bucket, which was originally used in a water well on an Indiana farm. Indiana and Michigan State play for the Old Brass Spittoon. In my senior year, we started the tradition of playing Ohio State for a live turtle; it was called Illibuck. They figured that turtles live long lives and we anticipated playing Ohio State for a long time, so the choice of the animal made sense. However, traveling between Champaign and Columbus proved to be too much for Illibuck and he died after two years. Since then, they've used a carved, wooden replica instead."

"Seeing how that rivalry has gone, they could probably go back to using a live turtle again," I say. "It wouldn't have to leave Columbus very often."

"Ouch," says the Ghost. "Sad, but true."

"Hey, we need to pick a game to go to," he says. "There are some terrific rivalries out there: Michigan and Ohio State, USC and Notre Dame, Army against Navy. Any thoughts?"

"How about Alabama versus Auburn?" I answer. "That's a great one down South."

"Excellent idea!" Red says as he jumps up from his chair. "Let's go check out the Iron Bowl!"

"Belvedere, are you with us?" I ask.

We look over and Belvedere is sound asleep in his chair.

"I think all the excitement was more than he could handle. Should we wake him up?" I ask.

"No, he looks too comfortable," says Red. "We'll just leave him a note."

Snap!

• • •

In a flash we're standing at the intersection of College Street and Magnolia Avenue, better known as Toomer's Corner, where the City of Auburn and its namesake university come together. Toomer's Corner is where Tigers fans gather to celebrate the school's victories and carry on their famous tradition of rolling the trees with toilet paper.

If you live in the state of Alabama, the battle lines are clearly drawn. You're either Roll Tide or War Eagle. Whether you went to one of those two schools or not, you must pick a side. With no major pro sports teams in the state, Auburn and Alabama get all the attention year-round. They say football is like a religion down South and many say it's more important. Bear Bryant said about the rivalry, "Nothing matters more than beating that cow college on the other side of the state." Trying to describe the animosity between the two schools is a waste of time; you need to live it 365 days a year to truly understand it. Alabama versus Auburn is just plain hate.

It's a beautiful fall day on the Plains and ESPN's College GameDay is here doing their weekly roadshow, signifying that this year's Iron Bowl is one of the country's marquee matchups of the day. The game will determine the winner of the SEC West division and the right to play in the conference championship. There is a huge, exuberant crowd gathered around the set.

"I've always wanted to see College GameDay in person," I say to Red. "I never thought I'd be dead when it happened."

"Better late than never," he says. "At least now we have unrestricted access behind the scenes."

Since it started in 1987, ESPN College GameDay has grown to become one of the most well-known traditions in college football. I've been watching the show as long as I can remember and wouldn't start a college football Saturday without it.

Red and I make ourselves comfortable on the set and watch the show as they review the lineup of the day's key games and news from across the country. I wish these guys knew that the man their network named in 2008 as the greatest college football player of all time is sitting right next to them on stage. I know they'd be thrilled to meet the Galloping Ghost.

During the breaks, Red and I look for ways to pass the time. As a joke, I suggest we play the hand slap game. Red says he doesn't know it but wants to learn so I go along.

"The version I grew up playing," I explain, "has one person hold their hands out in front of them, palms together, fingers straight and arms slightly bent at the elbow. The other person is facing them with their hands in the same position and the fingertips of both players almost touching. The object of the game is for the slapper to use either one of his hands to slap the back of the other person's hands before they can pull them away. If the slapper connects, then they go again. If they miss, then you switch roles. If the slappee pulls their hands away three times when a slap hasn't been attempted, then the slappee receives a penalty slap."

We do rock, paper, scissors to determine who will slap first and Red throws paper, which covers my rock. That ends up being a bad break for me. Turns out Red is lightning fast and can't miss. He's slapping me every time he swings no matter how fast I move. I start pulling my hands out at the slightest twitches and the penalty slaps he's taking are agonizing. Who would have thought this old-timer could be so fast? I think out of pity, Red takes a lazy swing and misses. Finally, I get some relief. The searing pain on the back of my hands almost causes them to go numb. I shake them out to try and bring some feeling back in them. At last it's my turn and I've got to make this count. Time for a little payback. I'm laser focused and with cat-like quickness I take a swing and connect with — nothing but air, a full whiff. Red chuckles a little and says to try again. I take another swing and another miss. I go again, same result. It's uncanny how quick his reflexes are, and he's got over fifty years on me. It's almost supernatural.

"What's your secret?" I ask. "How is it that you're so good at the games we play? You couldn't miss at cornhole and now the same with hand slap."

"It's pretty simple. I have a lot more experience as a ghost than you do. We haven't really been playing on a level field."

"What do you mean?"

"You're playing the game just like you would when you were alive. Remember, we can create anything we want as spirits. You're trying to do your best to win, right? I'm just thinking I can't lose, and I don't. That's the difference. Now that you know the secret, it's a whole new ballgame."

"Got it, thanks. Let's go again."

"The show's coming back," he says. "Let's pick it up during the next break."

The ESPN crew is talking about the Auburn and Alabama rivalry and some of the greatest games of the past. Lee Corso, who has experienced most of the major rivalries across the country says, "Alabama versus Auburn is the most intense, most competitive and best rivalry in all of college football."

Players like Joe Namath and Ken Stabler for Alabama and Bo Jackson and Pat Sullivan for Auburn have starred in the Iron Bowl which has produced some incredible games. They cut to a film clip from 1985 when Alabama is down by one point with six seconds remaining and they kick a fifty-two-yard field goal to win. In 2010, Alabama is ahead 24–0 in the second quarter and Cam Newton guides Auburn all the way back to a 28–27 victory on their way to winning the national championship. However, the most unbelievable game in the rivalry is the 2013 Iron Bowl, known as the Kick Six game. Alabama was the two-time defending national champion, ranked number one in the country with an 11-0 record coming into the game against fourth ranked Auburn at 10-1. The winner goes to the SEC championship game and a potential shot at the national championship game. With the score tied 28–28, Alabama drives to Auburn's thirty-nine-yard line with one second left on the clock. Bama sets up for a fifty-seven-yard field goal attempt and Auburn's Chris Davis goes back deep in his own end zone to cover. The kick is short of the goal post and Davis catches the ball about nine yards deep in the end zone. He runs it out and takes it all the way back through a slow-to-react Alabama team and scores the winning touchdown, one of the most miraculous plays in college football history.

ESPN goes to a break again, and I suggest to Red we try a different game, something a little less painful. I get a piece of paper and fold it up into a small triangle for finger football. The GameDay desk is open so we sit down and I go over the rules. Red loses the coin toss and must kick off to me. He flicks a good kick that stops a couple of inches from my edge of the table. I take over on offense and have four downs to either score a touchdown or kick a field goal. The ball lies flat on the table and I flick it so that it slides toward his end. After my second shot I'm about three inches from his edge of the table. This is a tough shot because it's very short and I need to flick the ball so that it stops with some part of the ball hanging over the edge to score a touchdown. If I hit it too hard and it falls off the table, Red takes over on offense. You can't nudge or push the ball; it must be a flick of the finger, generally using your thumb and index finger to make it a legal shot. I line up and make a perfect spin shot that stops with one of the ball's corners hanging over the edge.

"Touchdown!" I shout.

Finally, a little redemption! I just scored a touchdown against the Galloping Ghost. His advice to me is paying off.

Red makes a finger goalpost pointing his thumbs together and his index fingers straight up. I set the ball on its edge and flick it between the uprights; it hits Red right in the face, 7–0.

We are going back and forth having a blast in a very competitive game. The show is about to resume for its final segment and the crew takes their seats back at the desk. However, Red and I are engaged in an intense battle that we are now calling the Finger Bowl and we can't stop the game. ESPN goes live on the air and we have scrunched down to the end of the table next to Kirk Herbstreit and continue our game. With each score and kick, we are having a great time howling and trash talking each other.

GameDay host and Alabama alum Rece Davis announces it's time for the crew to make their picks of the day's games and Auburn alumnus Charles Barkley arrives as the celebrity guest picker wearing a "We Want Bama" shirt. They're picking through all the games, but meanwhile I'm leading Red 35–33 as he shanked two early extra points. The ESPN crew is almost ready to do their final pick of the day for the Alabama vs. Auburn game. We agree the next score wins. Red turns the ball over on downs choosing to go for a touchdown and comes up short instead of trying a game-winning field goal. I've got the ball and flick a long Hail Mary shot from my side of the table that slides toward Red's end. It crosses the edge and spins a couple of times before it comes to a stop. Touchdown! Game over. We're shouting and high-fiving each other. What a game! I finally beat him in something.

We kick back and watch the end of the show. Desmond Howard picks Alabama to win; Herbstreit picks the Tide as well. Sir Charles is next; his pick is obvious but hilarious.

"A few years ago, it was the Kick Six," he says. "Today, it's going to be the Kick Ass! Auburn wins!"

Everyone busts up laughing and the crowd goes wild. Lee Corso has to follow that and needs a few seconds to collect himself. The best tradition of the show is Corso's pick at the end when he puts on the headgear worn by the mascot of the school he thinks will win. He picks Alabama and puts on the headgear belonging to Big Al, the school's elephant mascot. The Auburn crowd unleashes an onslaught of boos.

• • •

It's getting close to game time and we head over to the stadium. It's a packed house, but we always have unrestricted VIP access wherever we want to go.

"Let's go up and see War Eagle before the game starts," says Red.

We find the imposing bird in his cage high up at the release point in the stadium.

A group of fans is gathered around his enclosure and one of the handlers announces, "You'll notice that Nova, the school's golden eagle, is not here today. He was diagnosed with a heart condition and is out of action until he recuperates, but we are fortunate to have Spirit, our magnificent bald eagle, filling in for us today.

"Here at Auburn University, eagles have been an inspirational symbol of strength, courage and freedom for over one hundred years," he continues. "A live War Eagle has made appearances on the team's sideline as far back as the 1930s and in the year 2000, the school started the awe-inspiring tradition of letting the bird loose to fly free around the stadium prior to kickoff."

One of the fans asks, "How did the War Eagle tradition get started?"

"The school offers up a few different versions about its origin," he says. "The most popular is that in 1892, a Civil War veteran was in the stands watching a game and he had brought an eagle with him. The legend says that he found the bird on a battlefield and kept it as a pet. During the game, the bird broke loose and started to soar around the field. Tigers fans were inspired by the bird's majestic flight along with Auburn's play on the field and began a battle cry, calling out "War Eagle," and the tradition was born. Tragically, at the end of the game, the bird took a dive toward the ground and died in a fatal crash."

Red and I introduce ourselves to the steely-eyed bird and ask if she wouldn't mind us tagging along on her pregame flight. With a name like Spirit, how could she refuse? She tells us to shrink down to fit on her shoulders and climb aboard. We position ourselves for departure and off we go. The great bird effortlessly glides over the roaring crowd. Soaring on the wings of this eagle is surreal; it feels as if everything is in slow motion.

Spirit circles around the stadium and floats gracefully down to a perfect landing at mid-field where her handler awaits. Kick-off is moments away.

• • •

The Iron Bowl ends up a gem for Auburn. The Tigers pull off a 26–14 upset victory, which clinches the division title and sends them to the conference championship next week.

After the game, we follow the crowd to Toomer's Corner to watch the post-game festivities. We hover above the famous intersection to watch the celebration as thousands of fans have gathered after Auburn's hard-fought victory. All the campus trees near the corner, along with the light poles and virtually every other stationary object in the area, are covered with toilet paper streamers making the area look like it had just been hit by a blizzard.

"What a great time!" says Red. "How about we head back to the Grotto and check on Belvedere?"

"I'd say it's about time for his wake-up call," I reply.

Snap!

12

HELP!

Back at the Grotto, we find Belvedere has already awoken from his football-induced coma.

"I owe you gentlemen an apology for my rude behavior," he says. "Falling asleep is inexcusable; I'm thoroughly embarrassed."

"Don't give it a second thought," I say. "We were going to wake you before we left, but you looked so comfortable we couldn't do it."

"I'm afraid my journey back home did me in. I just wasn't able to keep my eyes open any longer.

"To make amends, I prepared a treat for you gentlemen," he says, setting a large silver platter down on the table. "Baked Alaska with Cherries Jubilee. I hope you enjoy it."

"Belvedere, you never cease to amaze," says Red. "That looks delicious."

He serves up the mouth-watering combination of ice cream and cake covered in meringue, then pours the cherries and brandy over it and lights it on fire. We could barely wait for the flame to go out before gorging ourselves on the rich dessert.

"It's a good thing we don't have to worry about watching our weight anymore," says Red. "The way Belvedere feeds us around here, we'd all be over three hundred pounds if we were still on earth."

"Are you ready to head over to the camp with us?" I ask.

"Most assuredly, Mr. Kyle. I look forward to it."

Looking at Belvedere in his butler's uniform I mention, "It's a pretty casual environment over there. You might feel more comfortable with a change of clothes." Before he has a chance to think about it, I snap a crisp pair of khakis and a sharp-looking polo shirt on him. His expression is priceless. He looks as if he'd been suddenly stripped to his underwear. Red and I struggle to keep from laughing.

"Why . . . " he stammers, "I can't remember the last time I wasn't in my uniform. It feels so strange."

"You look great, Belvedere, like a new man," I say, popping a full-length mirror in front of him.

"You'll fit right in at camp," says Red. "Let's go!"

Snap!

• • •

Standing in our penthouse offices, I walk our old friend out to the balcony overlooking the entire campus. "Welcome to Camp Grange, Belvedere," I proudly proclaim while pointing out some of our state-of-the-art facilities. "How do you like our new digs?"

"Very impressive, sir."

"Red, how would you like to show Belvedere around the

place? Give him a sense of what we do here."

"Excellent idea! Let's go pal; allow me to give you the grand tour."

• • •

While the two of them are gone, I begin to think about Dr. Charcot and his team. Before long, they're going to have the final solutions for CTE, but it will take forever before it will have any impact on earth. Something has to be done.

Many times, earlier in my life, whenever I was faced with a difficult situation, I would think about my father and wonder how he might have dealt with the dilemma. When I was growing up, no matter the problem, Dad would always seem to come up with the solution.

I remember back one time when I was about eight. I was playing in front of my house and our neighbor from across the street, Mr. Loomis, came out of his house, bare-chested and fully tattooed, waving a baseball bat around and yelling incoherently. Loomis was usually a pretty quiet guy, but when he was on drugs, he just seemed to lose his mind; Dad said he used angel dust. This wasn't a new occurrence; we'd seen Loomis in these drug-fueled rants before, usually ending with the police hauling him away. One time, it took four cops to finally wrestle him to the ground after using their batons, pepper spray and a taser to slow him down.

This time he was staggering aimlessly around his driveway swinging the bat around like he was swatting flies. It was funny but sad, and you couldn't help wondering what he imagined was after him. Suddenly he stopped dead in his tracks and stared straight in my direction. I took a couple of steps backward and he began to head my way. Dad immediately came out our front door and called for me to come inside. I hustled in and went around to watch from our living room window. My father cautiously walked out to approach him in the middle of the street. It seemed as dangerous as walking up to a wild bull. After a few minutes, appearing to have some sort of hypnotic effect, he was able to get Loomis to calm down. My dad put his hand out and Loomis handed him the bat. They turned and walked back to his house.

They had been in there quite a while and I started to worry if everything was okay. A few minutes later, the door opened and my father calmly returned home. We never heard another thing from Loomis that day and never saw him in that condition again; it was remarkable. Loomis eventually got help to kick his addiction problems and was able to turn his life around. Dad said he was tired of standing by, watching our neighbor go through another ordeal with the police. He thought he could help talk him through it and he was right.

Unfortunately, whenever I think of that day or other times my father's inspiration began to provide me guidance, a wave of resentment would inevitably hijack my thoughts, pulling me into a dark place. Memories of all the love and respect I had for my father would vanish into pain and anger. How could someone so capable and heroic fail to overcome the obstacles that would cause him to take his own life? How could he abandon my mother and me to fend for ourselves when we depended on him so much, when we loved him so much?

Moving forward without him left a deep depression that robbed me of hope and optimism. It became too easy to feel like giving up and too difficult to gather the energy and courage to care about tomorrow. I used to fall into these dark holes so often I needed to force myself not to let my thoughts wander toward my father; the lows could be very difficult to dig out of. When I was young, I could always count on him to be there for me, but suddenly when he was gone, I had to grow up quickly and learn to rely on myself to solve life's problems.

• • •

Suddenly, an idea flashes in my head. "Jessica, can you hear me?" I call out.

To my surprise she instantly replies, "Yes Kyle, what's on your mind?"

"Wow, how do you do that? It's like you've been here the whole time."

"You and Red are two of my top priorities. No matter where I am, I hear your calls loud and clear. How can I help?"

"Jessica, you and your team have been extremely supportive of our efforts getting the camp going, recruiting talent and giving us everything we need. I can't thank you enough. We are making great progress and we're happy that they appreciate our efforts upstairs, but I've come to realize that what we are doing here, especially Dr. Charcot's group, simply takes too long before it gets down to earth and does any good. The doctors' breakthroughs with CTE are a real game-changer. Why can't we get down there now and put their discoveries to work right away? We need to change the system. Can you help us?"

"Kyle, you and Red are doing a tremendous job here. In fact, you're exceeding everyone's expectations. I can empathize with your frustration, but you need to try to understand the big picture. In heaven, things move at a much different pace. A decade on earth is like a grain of sand through heaven's hourglass. The realities of purgatory and reincarnation have been in existence since the dawn of man and that process was put in place for a reason. Purgatory spirits cannot take it upon themselves to interfere with the course of human events.

"The grand design of God's plan is so infinitely complex; it is light years beyond the comprehension of the human spirit. Everyone that goes through purgatory, enlightened by the lessons they learn here, must ascend to heaven prior to being reincarnated on earth. While in heaven, those souls must be purified for rebirth and imprinted with their new destinies according to the master plan. We can't short-circuit the process."

"I understand what you're saying, but surely there must be something that can be done. Can't you go upstairs and plead my case?"

"Kyle, I want to help you any way I can, but you're asking the impossible. These things are cast in stone."

"For the good of the game and the people who play it, please help! Right now, there are people needlessly suffering from the effects of this disease that would benefit from our discoveries. I beg you; we need to get this down to earth as soon as it's ready."

"Okay Kyle, I hear you," she says. "Look, I can't give you any guarantees, but I'll go upstairs and do everything I can to get this changed. Keep your fingers crossed!"

13

Money

"How was the tour?" I inquire as Red and Belvedere return to the office.

"Splendid, sir. You fellows have quite an operation here."

"Anything jump out that you might want to get involved with?" I ask.

"The pub . . . I believe you call it the Gridiron," he says. "I suppose that might be something I should consider. However, it's a pretty lively place. I think it might be a bit overwhelming for me."

"I can understand that," says Red. "It's a really busy place with a lot of colorful characters cycling through. That might not be a great fit for you."

"All the other areas for coaches, players and referees—I'm afraid I'd be completely lost." Belvedere pauses for a moment. "Gentlemen, I appreciate what you're doing for me, but I'm a butler. It's what I've done my entire life; it's what I love doing. I'm an old dog that's not interested in learning any new tricks. If you don't mind, I'd prefer to just continue my duties as a butler serving you both here in the executive suite."

"That's music to my ears," says Red. "I couldn't be happier that you still want to stick around with us, old friend."

"I admire you for that, Belvedere," I say. "You know what you want to do and you love doing it. We can expand the offices and put in a bar and fireplace and some of the other creature comforts to make everyone feel more at home. How does that sound?"

"That would be wonderful, sir. Also, if you don't mind, I'd prefer to wear my butler uniform as well."

"By all means my good man," says Red. "You'll add a special touch of class to the place. Now how about rustling up some coffee for us? I could use a pick-me-up."

"Right away, Mr. Red."

As Belvedere shuffles off, the TV monitors around the office show an ESPN report talking about the recent NFL draft. The number one overall pick is expected to receive a contract worth about $35 million. Over $20 million of that will be paid upfront as a bonus just for the player to sign his name on the contract, before he ever plays a single down in the NFL.

"In my first year of pro football I earned about a hundred and twenty-five thousand dollars and that was *after* I played nineteen games over a sixty-seven-day period," Red says. "They ran us into the ground."

"Times have really changed," I reply.

"I was by far the highest-paid player in the game and that kind of money was considered a fortune back then. In those days, you could buy a brand-new car for around four hundred bucks, a suit of clothes for ten and a meal at a good restaurant for less than a dollar. Most of the other players in the league at that time were earning about twenty-five to a hundred dollars a game. What do you think that hundred and twenty-five thousand from 1925 would be worth in today's money?"

"Hmm, factoring in an average of about three percent inflation per year over ninety-four years, I'm thinking about $1.8 million today," I reply.

"Off the field, I made an additional eighty-five thousand from endorsements and a movie deal."

"That would be worth another $1.2 million today," I say. "Three million dollars is still a pretty good income these days. The money in the game has grown exponentially and the players deserve everything they get, considering the risks of injury and the long odds of making it in pro football. Fewer than two percent of college football players make it to the NFL."

"When I was growing up," says the Ghost, "money was always in short supply for my family. As a kid, everyday life was a real challenge. By the time I entered high school, my father and brother and I were living in a small apartment above a store in the middle of Wheaton. We were so poor, all I did was go to school, study, and play sports. There was no money for dating or any kind of social life. For me, football was really an escape from a difficult childhood. When I went out for football in high school, we couldn't afford to buy a new helmet and cleats, so I scraped together enough money to buy a used helmet from a former student. When we had games, I borrowed cleats from other teammates who weren't playing. My entire freshman year, I never once played in a pair of shoes that fit me."

"Things were really difficult for my mother and me as well after my father died," I reply. "He didn't leave her with any life insurance money and there wasn't much in savings either. She was determined to keep our house and worked two jobs to keep a roof over our heads. I used to mow lawns around the neighborhood to help bring in some money. When I was old enough, I got a job at McDonald's flipping burgers."

"During the summer after my freshman year in high school," says Red, "I started working on an ice truck delivering blocks of ice to help support the family. I was making around thirty-seven dollars a week, working twelve hours a day, six days a week. It worked out to a little more than fifty cents an hour for tough physical labor hauling huge blocks of ice on my shoulder going from house to house.

"I worked on that truck for eight summers to help put myself through college. That was in the days before athletic scholarships existed to pay for a player's tuition, books, room and board. After my big sophomore season at Illinois, the newspapers and magazines were running a photo of me with a block of ice slung over my shoulder. They nicknamed me, 'The Wheaton Iceman.' I could have easily found other work that required very little effort after that breakout season. It was common for college players to have jobs that only required them to show up on paydays to collect their checks. Instead, I chose to continue to work on the ice truck each summer because of the strength and conditioning I gained from the demanding labor. I felt it gave me an enormous edge over other players heading into training camp each fall. I was so committed to that summer training regimen that I even returned to work on the ice truck after my first year in pro football. The only difference was that this summer, I drove up to work each day in my fifty-five-hundred-dollar Lincoln Phaeton."

"Man, that must have been some car!" I say.

"It was beautiful. My boss, Mr. Thompson, used to ask me to park around back. He joked that the car made it confusing as to who was working for whom. Looking back, I probably should have been smarter about my spending, but I had been poor all my life and I really wanted to splurge. I should have listened to Babe Ruth. The first time I met him he said, 'Kid, I'll give you a little bit of advice. Get the dough while the gettin' is good and don't pick up too many checks.' I made so much that first year, you just think the money's going to keep rolling in. I thought I was on my way to making a million dollars."

"Tell me about when you made the jump to pro ball."

"At the start of my senior year at Illinois, I was approached by a fellow named C.C. Pyle, a local theater owner in Champaign, who gave guys on the football team free passes for the movies. Pyle was an opportunistic chap who saw my potential to make big money playing pro football. He seized the opportunity to earn my trust and hooked me with the idea of earning one hundred thousand dollars or more in the pros. That amount of money was staggering to me and meant the chance to climb out of poverty and help my family. After giving it some thought, the offer was simply too good to pass up and I entered into a handshake agreement with Pyle to act as my business representative. All the while, I had to be concerned with maintaining my eligibility for the upcoming season; an agreement of this nature could potentially jeopardize my standing on the team. Pyle and I were careful to keep our arrangement under wraps until after I played my final game for Illinois."

"That sounds like a heck of an opportunity," I say. "However, from what I recall, the schools weren't too happy to see their players go on to play professionally."

"The college football establishment hated the idea of pro football," says the Ghost. "The colleges had developed the game and fostered its enormous popularity. They didn't like the thought of competition from the pro ranks and the threat of losing fans to the fledgling league. Also, the college academic types weren't pleased with the idea that a big-time athlete could play three years of college football, then turn pro and make more money in a few months than a professor makes in an entire year. Needless to say, I wasn't encouraged to pursue a career in the NFL. After I finished playing football at Illinois, I was expected to hang up my cleats and go into coaching or become a referee, maybe get a newspaper job, but not lower myself to the scourge of pro football. I'd have been more popular with the colleges if

I had joined Capone's mob in Chicago rather than the Bears."

"What did your coach think about all this?" I ask. "He obviously had to have known about your family's financial situation. You did so much for his program; did he support you?"

"Bob Zuppke," he says, "was a staunch advocate of the college establishment and believed that professional football was beneath someone of my stature. He told me, 'Keep away from professionalism and you'll be another Walter Camp. Football isn't a game to be played for money.' I couldn't agree with his double standard and I told him so. 'You get paid for coaching, Zup. Why should it be wrong for me to get paid for playing?' It just didn't make sense to me to be so good at something and then be told I have to give it up after I leave college. Especially with the opportunity out there to make so much money and wipe out the financial pressures my father and I were under."

"As I recall, the NFL was on pretty shaky ground in those early days," I mention.

"The league was only a few years old and was struggling with poor attendance, minimal newspaper coverage and small player salaries, but the product on the field was good. Many of the players were former college stars who still played for the love of the game despite the low pay. Back in those days, there was no amateur draft by the NFL. Prospective players were free to negotiate with whatever teams they were interested in playing for. The best players ended up going to the best teams, who could pay the most. The concept of competitive balance hadn't taken hold yet in the NFL, and the first draft wouldn't take place for another eleven years, in 1936."

"How did you end up with the Bears?"

"After I agreed to let Charlie Pyle represent me, he arranged a meeting with the Bears' owners, George Halas and Dutch Sternaman. They were both former Illinois players and the Bears were the most logical pro team for me. Pyle told them that after I played my final game for Illinois, I would be ready to sign a contract to play professionally. But not only was Pyle pitching me, he also was proposing his own plans for the Bears to embark on a national exhibition tour. They had a marathon negotiating session and finally reached an agreement: the Bears would split the gate revenue fifty-fifty with Pyle and me and from our half, I would get sixty percent and Pyle forty.

"Once we had that verbal agreement in place with the Bears, Pyle went on the road to set up the tour. Amazingly, the agreement to play for the Bears and the upcoming exhibition tour was kept quiet during Illinois' season, which allowed me to play without any repercussions."

"That's remarkable, even for that era," I say. "It wouldn't have been even remotely possible in today's digital age and social media."

"Yep, we got lucky. Immediately following our final game against Ohio State, I announced on the field that I was leaving school to play for the Bears. The next day I signed a contract with Pyle to act as my manager and a few hours later I signed my contract with the Bears. A few months after that I was a very rich young man."

"What a great story!" I say. "You had your shot and hit a home run. It makes me think of what Barry Switzer said: 'Some people are born on third base and go through life thinking they hit a triple.' You started with nothing and came all the way around to score."

"Thanks, pal, but it wasn't all smooth sailing. Even with my windfall in pro football, I hit a rough patch financially after I injured my knee. While I was out of the game, I struggled to pay the bills. I went back to Hollywood to make another film, which turned out to be a dud, and then resorted to doing a six-month vaudeville tour trying to make ends meet."

"Sorry to interrupt, gentlemen," says Belvedere, shuffling in, "but this message was just delivered. It looks important."

"Ah, a note from upstairs," I say, noticing the unmistakable scroll of angel parchment in his hand. "Hmm, it looks like we have our first occupants in the Ivory Tower: a school president and an athletic director recently killed in a plane crash. Sounds interesting; shall we go welcome them aboard?"

"I'm right behind you," says the Ghost.

Snap!

14

"Mo Money Mo Problems"

My original plan for the Ivory Tower was to be a place where wayward school administrators would be sent to contemplate their corruptive misconduct and seek redemption. The angels were in favor of the concept but had a somewhat different vision. Rather than a communal think tank of spiritual reparation, the Tower was to be stone-cold solitary confinement. Corruption is not taken lightly upstairs. Perpetrators would be stripped of all liberties typically afforded purgatory spirits and sent to the Tower until further notice. Whereas the rest of Camp Grange was a rehabilitative stopover for spirits on their way to heaven, the Tower was set aside as an exile for administrative types whose ultimate fate has yet to be decided.

• • •

We meet our two new arrivals waiting in a dreary, windowless interview room. According to my notes, Ronald Ainsworth was a long-time university president and Gregory Metzger was his head of athletics.

"Gentlemen, my name is Kyle and this is my colleague Harold. Please have a seat."

"Where are we?" asks Ainsworth.

"You are in a special area within purgatory," I reply. "It's called the Ivory Tower. Harold and I run this facility."

"How did we end up here?" Ainsworth persists.

"When you died, it was determined that you weren't ready for heaven so you were sent here."

"Well I'll be damned," remarks Metzger. "So heaven really does exist. I never believed it—always thought it was just some old superstition. Tell me, what's it like?"

"I couldn't tell you," says Red. "We've never been."

"Well how do you know it really exists?" asks Metzger.

"Let's just say we've been around long enough to know for sure," says the Ghost.

"By the way, you look really familiar," says Metzger. "Have we met before?"

"No, I don't think so," says Red.

"I could swear I know you."

"I get that a lot. I just have one of those familiar faces," says Red, who likes to avoid getting bogged down in fan interaction with our clientele.

"I understand you guys died in a plane crash," I say. "What happened?"

"We were flying in our school's Gulfstream to a fundraising event when we hit some bad weather," says Metzger. "The pilot said we were coming up on some extremely dense fog and they weren't equipped to fly through it. We were running late for the event and if they tried to go around it, we'd probably miss the entire thing, so we insisted they drop down and fly under it. We must have been flying too low to the ground because after a few minutes, I think we clipped something with one of the wings. It all happened so quickly. There was a horrific impact that suddenly caused the plane to jerk sideways. A gaping hole ripped open along the side of the cabin and the plane lunged into a downward spiral. I was thrown up against the ceiling but Ron was still belted into his seat. We locked eyes for an instant; I'll never forget that look of terror staring back. Within a few seconds, we hit the ground. All of us were killed instantly on impact as the plane exploded in a massive fireball.

"The next thing I remember, we're floating up above the crash site in the middle of nowhere. The two pilots disappeared in the fog and Ron and I ended up here."

"The whole thing was a nightmare I hoped to wake up from," says Ainsworth, "but never did."

"You guys must be pretty shaken up," I say. "Do you want some time to recuperate?"

Ainsworth looks over at Metzger, who gives him a *whatever* shrug, then says, "No, I think we're okay; we're probably more interested in what happens from here."

"Well, the first step is for you guys to figure out why you were sent to purgatory," I say.

The two glance at each other and then stare off in silence. Finally, Metzger chimes in, "I think it's got to have something to do with the money," he says. "Between skyrocketing TV contracts, sponsorships, big-money donors, luxury suites and ticket sales, there was just so much of it pouring into college football. Ron hired me to help build a plan for us to get as much of it as we could."

"It's remarkable," says Ainsworth, "to think that a game that had its beginnings as an intramural pastime played by college kids in the mid-1800s has grown into an industry that generates billions of dollars a year in revenue."

"I know the money out there is incredible," I remark. "I was chasing it myself when I worked in USC's athletic department."

"You're kidding!" says Metzger. "What a small world. How was it working for one of the blue bloods?"

"I was just a cog in the machine, but it amazed me that despite the tradition and success of our program, we consistently underachieved in monetizing our football program. We would usually rank about eighteenth in the country in football revenue while schools like Texas, Michigan, Alabama, and Ohio State led the way, bringing in tens of millions more each year. Of course, a lot of that has to do with being a part of the Pac-12, which always lags far behind some of the other major conferences."

"At least SC was one of the profitable programs," says Metzger. "You'd think with all that money flowing in, athletic departments would be swimming in profits, but only about twenty-five schools turn a profit in any given year. Even though schools in the Power Five are raking in the money, the majority are losing more money than ever. About sixty percent of the Power Five schools operate in the red. Everyone's caught up in a high-stakes game of spending on new facilities and coaches' salaries, chasing wins on the field and trying to gain a competitive edge in recruiting."

"It's an endless competition to build shiny new things that appeal to seventeen-year-old kids so they'll pick you instead of someone else," says Ainsworth.

"In addition to mega stadium renovations and private jets, schools are spending to create lavish resorts for their athletes," says Metzger, "everything from miniature golf courses to laser tag, bowling lanes, movie theaters, sand volleyball courts, barber shops, leisure pools, and lounges. One school decided it needed a new video board for its football stadium, so it installed an eleven-thousand-square-foot jumbotron. It's roughly the size of a five-story building, the largest in college football. The nighttime glow from the board can be seen from nearly thirty miles away. The school said it would help recruit top athletes and sell tickets, so they spent fourteen million dollars on the project, even though their athletic department had a seventeen-million-dollar deficit the previous year."

"Athletic directors at money-losing departments justify their spending as being necessary to keep pace with the competition," says Ainsworth. "In spite of all the money coming in, most departments outspend their income and are forced to make up the difference by taking on debt, charging mandatory student fees, or getting bailed out by digging into their school's general fund. It costs many of the country's largest publicly-funded universities and their students millions of dollars."

"How is this allowed to happen?" asks Red.

"Athletic departments typically operate with a great deal of autonomy, free to spend whatever they bring in, and the administrations rarely prevent them from overspending," says Metzger. "It all dates back to the early days of the sport when Camp and Stagg pioneered the commercialization of college sports. They created autonomous athletic departments that had little accountability to their schools' academic administration, faculty and students. They worked with their school presidents and built departments that had tremendous influence within their institutions and were free to use school resources to generate extra income for themselves and their departments. Athletic directors from other schools saw what was going on and pushed their schools to adopt similar policies and the model spread across the country."

"Of course, another reason these departments overspend is because the people in charge are playing with other people's money and they have limited motivation to reduce costs to stay in the black," says Ainsworth. "Also, a lot of the time they jump ship before things come crashing down. Then they leave the mess for someone else to clean up."

Ainsworth pauses for a moment and then mentions, "You said earlier that *we* need to figure out why we're here. I suppose it's not very difficult to understand. We weren't exactly choir boys down there."

"Anything you'd like to share?" I ask.

"If we're being totally honest here, *our* plan was to jump ship before things blew apart at our school. Greg was going to be off to a better job somewhere else and I was going to be retired on a beach somewhere sipping umbrella drinks. I guess we can come clean; none of it matters anymore."

"I beg to differ with you," says Red. "It all matters. That's why you're in purgatory. What you did down there and how you feel about it now will go a long way toward determining where you go from here. I would highly recommend that you fellas be completely candid and tell us your story."

Ainsworth proceeds, "It started when I was appointed president of our university. The state thought they were putting me out to pasture when they sent me to run that place, but I knew I had some good years ahead of me and decided to make the most of it. When I took over, our campus was still mostly a commuter school. It was an afterthought in the system, sorely lacking any real identity and badly in need of a makeover. Trying to get money out of the state was like pulling teeth so I started exploring other ways to generate funding. Athletics, specifically football, seemed like a good place to start and since I loved the sport, I decided to focus our resources on building up the program to put the school on the map. The plan was to turn it into a juggernaut and make a lot of money along the way.

"To accomplish that, I needed the right athletic director. Greg was an up-and-comer in an athletic department at a small private school back east that was referred to me by a mutual friend. He was looking for an opportunity to spread his wings and I thought he might be a great fit. To say this was a ground-floor opportunity was overselling it. This was more like starting in the basement without any stairs where you have to claw your way up to get to the ground floor. But I guess I'm a pretty good salesman because after a couple of meetings, he was sold on my vision and signed on.

"From there, I turned over most of our board and hand-picked the new trustees among friends and loyal supporters. There was a strong desire among the city's wealthy to have a winning football program and they were willing to foot the bill, so we got to work raising money. Over time, we brought in millions for stadium renovations, new practice facilities and coaches' salaries. The football program was the front porch to the university and more wins meant increased donor support, more freshman applications and better applicants. We were designing a blueprint for building an institution of higher learning out of our athletics program."

"In addition to generating the money," says Metzger, "my mandate was to ensure the football team produced on the field. I wanted a head coach that wasn't going to cost us a lot but had the desire to build a program from the ground up and recruit the talent to compete at a high level. That meant I was looking for someone who was overlooked and undervalued in the industry. I knew of a guy that was down and out of football with some baggage in his past, a kind of rough-around-the-edges type, and I thought he was worth the gamble. Ray Whittaker knew the game inside out: fundamentals, technique, execution and discipline. He could teach and motivate, was a great strategist and tactician and could recruit. No other schools were willing to touch him. He had a show-cause order from the NCAA a few years earlier and hadn't been able to get back in the game even after it expired. There were alcohol problems and domestic violence issues in his younger days that also scared people off, but I always felt he had the talent to be a great coach. Our program didn't get much scrutiny from the press or the community. The board was all in our corner so we could pretty much bring in whomever we wanted, as long as people believed we were going to win. After all, America is the land of second chances and winning washes away a lot of sins.

"I brought Ray in for an interview and laid things out. This was a win at all cost situation; we were going to build something out of nothing, and we weren't going to let anything stand in our way—absolutely nothing. We would get the money and spend it to make this happen.

"Ray said he had cleaned up the problems in his past and

was desperate for an opportunity to get back into college football and prove himself. I was offering a chance for him to be a head coach. Granted, it was at the bottom of the FBS at a school no one had ever heard of, but it was his shot at redemption. I wanted him and his staff to focus on the Xs and Os, build the best team possible and I would put people around the program to take care of the off-the-field stuff. I expected them to recruit relentlessly and let me know whenever there was a kid they wanted who might need a little something extra in order to commit to the program. I had boosters lined up that would pay to grease the skids with any player or family to steer them our way. They would also take care of any high school or seven-on-seven coaches that we needed to persuade players to join our program.

"I had staff in place doing the dirty work to keep players eligible with fictitious classes and tutors on hand to complete assignments and write papers. I put a couple of retired detectives on the payroll to keep an eye on the players and get them out of trouble with local law enforcement whenever necessary."

"Sounds like you had everything figured out," Red says sarcastically.

"If you ain't cheatin', you ain't tryin'," says Metzger. "As it turned out, Coach Whittaker was the right guy. He's building a solid program down there and he only cost us a mid-six-figure salary. We weren't competing with the Power Five schools yet, but we were able to get players and coaches and build facilities that allowed us to start winning consistently at the Group of Five level. We were flying under the radar from a national perspective, but we were a program on the rise in the lower echelon of the FBS and I was positioning us to get an invitation to a Power Five conference in the next couple of years."

"We had laid the foundations and were on the verge of breaking through to the big time," says Ainsworth. "As the results on the football field improved and the donor support grew, I continued to get both our salaries bumped up well beyond the range of our peers. We kept it pretty low profile, but I was making about twenty times the annual salary of a full-time professor and Greg was bringing in a salary approaching that of a Power Five AD. I even arranged for us to be paid gross-ups on our salaries, which was basically paying our taxes for us.

"It was a great setup. In addition to having our board in my back pocket, I ran the foundation that controlled the school's endowment and would regularly dip into it to pay for virtually any expense or luxury I saw fit. There was a lot of fuzzy accounting going on to keep things under wraps. One time I had one of our accountants tell me that at the rate we were going, if we kept tapping the endowment, it would eventually deplete the entire fund."

"What did you do?" I ask.

"I fired him on the spot!" Ainsworth barks.

"Okay," Red interrupts, "I think we've heard enough."

"Hey, you told us to open up and spill the beans," says Metzger.

"You're right, and this is an important first step," I respond. "There's no mystery why you're here."

"What happens now?" asks Ainsworth.

"For now, you'll both be confined to separate quarters until further notice," I reply.

"We're being locked up, like prisoners?" Metzger pleads. "I thought you guys were going to help us."

"Our role here is to help spirits move on to heaven," I reply. "In fact, this entire facility was specifically designed to help spirits that were involved in college football enter the Pearly Gates. We work with players, coaches, trainers, referees and fans; everyone eventually moves on to heaven. However, this Tower is unique. It was set up as a holding facility for administrators who were found to be corrupting the game. That level of dishonesty is not tolerated upstairs, and it has become a top priority to clean up the game. We have been informed that spirits sent to the Tower don't have a clear path for redemption to enter heaven."

"What does that mean?" asks Ainsworth.

"We're not exactly sure. You're our first arrivals here, so you're kind of a test case. I think they're still trying to figure it out upstairs. But when they say you have no clear path to heaven, it seems like your only other options might be that you either spend eternity here or else get sent downstairs.

"You're saying we could end up in hell? For what *we* did? That's outrageous!" shouts Ainsworth.

"We don't make the rules here; we're just following orders," says Red.

"Who else can we talk to about this?" asks Ainsworth.

"I'm afraid we're all you've got right now," replies Red.

"That's just great," says Metzger sarcastically.

"Someone will be right in to take you to your quarters," I say. "In the meantime, I would seriously consider trying to find some genuine regret for the things you did and hope for the best. I'm sure we'll be talking again in the future. Good luck."

• • •

Walking down the hallway from the interview room, Red's shaking his head, "Can you believe those guys? I sure wouldn't want to be in their shoes."

"Yeah, I definitely feel like I could use a shower after that. Money can make people do crazy things."

Belvedere appears in the hallway. "Another message just arrived from upstairs, sir."

I unravel the scroll and read the brief note before angrily crumpling it up.

"Bad news?" asks Red.

"It's from Jessica. She obviously didn't want to tell me in person. It's this whole reincarnation thing. I asked her to go upstairs and plead for them to expedite things so our work doesn't take forever to get down to earth. She says she tried her best but they wouldn't budge; case closed.

"You know Red, I really appreciate you bringing me into this place and I absolutely enjoy what we're doing, but this is really frustrating. I need to get some air and cool off."

"Do you want some company, pal?

"No thanks, I'll be all right. I just need to go for a walk and clear my head. I'll meet you back at the office later."

15

The Great Eight

I return to the office and find Red slouched down in his chair, feet propped up on the desk, sound asleep. "Hey, wake up!" I say with a nudge. He barely opens one eye. "You're busted, my friend. You said you never sleep; you don't need it. I'm gone for a little while and everything grinds to a halt. What's up with that?"

The Ghost scratches his head and tries to rub the sleep out of his eyes. "I don't know what happened. With you not around stirring everything up, it was so quiet. I just dozed off."

"Relax, I'm givin' you a hard time. You deserve some rest, but not now. There's something I want to show you."

"You seem to be in a better mood," he says.

"Yeah, it was good to take a break—let off a little steam. I got a chance to work on something I've been wanting to tackle and I'd like to show you a little surprise. You ready?"

Snap!

I transport us to the entrance of The Great Eight.

"What do we have here?" asks the Ghost.

"It's the newest addition to Camp Grange: an immersive virtual tour of the greatest programs in college football history."

"You have got to get a life," he says.

"I know, but it's too late for that."

"What gave you this idea?" he asks.

"Everyone talks about the elite programs or the blue bloods of college football. Most of them immediately come to mind. We know where the list starts, but where does it end? Who's in and who's out? I wanted to clearly identify who they are, so I did some research. There are a lot of schools that have produced excellent programs throughout the history of the game. Some had their heydays in the early beginnings of the sport and then faded from national prominence. Others had successful runs but lack a track record of sustained success and longevity. When you start to analyze which schools have established the greatest programs of all time, you take into account accomplishments like national championships, conference championships, Heisman Trophy winners, consensus All-Americans, all-time win-loss record and winning percentage. After considering all the relevant information, a clear picture begins to emerge. There are eight schools that have set themselves apart from the rest of the field as the most outstanding in history. I wanted to recognize those programs and their most influential coaches, so I designed this tour for everyone that comes through Camp Grange."

"You created this place on your break?' asks Red.

"Yep," I reply.

"You have an interesting way of letting off steam, Kyle. Some people drink or do drugs while others punch or kick something. You, on the other hand, create a theme park attraction for college football—I love it."

We move into the main hall, where the walls are adorned with some of the most iconic images in college football history. There's an illustration of the Princeton and Rutgers game from November 6, 1869, Doug Flutie's "Miracle in Miami," Desmond Howard's end zone Heisman pose and Cal's stunning, multi-lateral touchdown run through the Stanford band to name a few. The entire ceiling is dedicated to the image of the Galloping Ghost sweeping around right end in his big game against Michigan. At the far end of the cavernous hall, we enter the portal to the tour and take our seats for the journey.

The lights fade until we're surrounded in total darkness. Moments later, off in the distance, we hear the faint but unmistakable sound of the Notre Dame Victory March. The fight song builds to a crescendo and a towering panorama of the iconic image of Notre Dame's legendary four-man backfield mounted on horseback fills our view. The music subsides as the voice of college football, Keith Jackson, begins, "Outlined against a blue-gray October sky, the Four Horsemen rode again. In dramatic lore they are known as Famine, Pestilence, Destruction and Death. These are only aliases. Their real names are Stuhldreher, Miller, Crowley and Layden.

"Grantland Rice wrote this lead for his coverage in the *New York Herald Tribune* describing Notre Dame's victory over Army in 1924. It became one of the most famous passages in the annals of sports journalism. The Irish went on to a perfect season and their first national championship led by the Four Horsemen, one of the greatest backfields in college football history."

"Nice touch using Keith Jackson," whispers Red. "How is the old coot?"

"I had to pull some strings to get him to narrate the tour, but he was happy to help. He wanted to be here to say hello but he's playing golf with Palmer, Eisenhower and Ford. He hoped you'd understand."

The Horsemen picture dissolves to an image of the father of Notre Dame football, Knute Rockne. He begins telling the deathbed tale of former player George Gipp, one of Notre Dame's greatest all-around players. Rockne says, "Gipp is lying in a hospital bed dying from strep throat and pneumonia just days after playing his final game for the school. Gipp tells me, 'I've got to go, Rock. It's all right. I'm not afraid. Sometime, Rock, when the team is up against it, when things are wrong, and the breaks are beating the boys, ask them to go in there with all they've got and win just one for the Gipper. I don't know where I'll be then, Rock. But I'll know about it, and I'll be happy.' A moment later Gipp was gone."

"Rockne waited eight years after Gipp's death before using this story in his halftime speech that inspired his underdog Irish team to an upset victory over a previously unbeaten Army team in 1928," says Jackson. "In the locker room, Rockne tells his players, 'The day before he died, George Gipp asked me to wait until the situation seemed hopeless—then ask a Notre Dame team to go out and beat Army for him. This is the day, and you are the team.'"

"Rockne was a helluva coach," says Red. "He won three national championships in his thirteen years as their head coach."

"He also won eighty-eight percent of his games, which is the highest career-winning percentage of any major college coach in history," I add.

"Unfortunately, we'll never know how great he could have been," says the Ghost. "He was only forty-three years old and had just won back-to-back national championships before dying in that plane crash. Tragic! He was just getting started."

We begin to soar on an aerial tour of the Notre Dame campus, which takes us over some of the country's most recognizable college landmarks. We get a bird's-eye view of the golden dome atop the school's main building and the thirteen-story-tall mosaic of Touchdown Jesus on the library building overlooking Notre Dame Stadium. We glide in for a close-up look at the Grotto of Our Lady of Lourdes, which is a scaled-down replica of the actual site in France, where it is said the Virgin Mary appeared to Saint Bernadette eighteen times in 1858.

"It's not exactly the campus saloon you envisioned as a young kid, is it?" jokes Red.

"Nope, but I am getting thirsty," I reply.

"Two ice-cold beers comin' right up," says the Ghost.

The scene shifts to a view of the Horseshoe at Ohio State where the Best Damn Band in the Land plays out its signature Script Ohio formation. Subbing in for the sousaphone player is Bob Hope, who comes out and dots the "i" in Ohio.

We move to a chalk talk where Woody Hayes expounds on his football philosophy. "When you pass the football," he says, "three things can happen and two of them are bad. I don't like the odds of success in the passing game. You have to run the football to win games. To move the ball and maintain possession, each play should gain at least three yards."

"Woody's conservative, ground-and-pound offensive philosophy came to be known as 'three yards and a cloud of dust,'" says Jackson. "It served him well. After taking over the Ohio State program in 1951, he led the Buckeyes for the next twenty-eight years, winning five national championships along with thirteen Big Ten Conference titles.

"The annual Ohio State vs. Michigan clash is considered one of the greatest rivalries in American sports. Woody had such disdain for his rivals from Michigan, he couldn't even bring himself to mention Michigan by name and started the trend of calling them 'that school up north.'"

"I once ran out of gas up north," says Woody. "I pushed my car back across the border into Ohio because I refused to buy gas in that state. I wouldn't give them one damn nickel of my money."

We flash to 1968 where Ohio State has a commanding

50–14 lead late in the game over Michigan. After the Buckeyes have scored their final touchdown, Woody decides to go for two but the play fails. Afterward, Hayes is asked why he went for two. "Because I couldn't go for three," he barks.

"Woody had a temper and a history of emotional and physical outbursts," says Jackson.

Woody recalls, "When I look in the mirror in the morning, I want to take a swing at me."

"Hayes also hated to lose, let alone having to account for it to the press," says Jackson.

"After losses or ties," says Hayes, "I usually conduct locker room interviews buck naked. I'm kind of an ugly guy so it clears out the locker room pretty fast."

"Woody's coaching career didn't end well," says Jackson. "His temper got the better of him during the 1978 Gator Bowl when he punched an opposing player from Clemson who had just intercepted a pass to seal a victory over the Buckeyes. I was calling the game that day on ABC and neither myself nor my broadcast partner Ara Parseghian were looking at the monitor so we both missed the punch, which was seen by millions on television. We just plain old whiffed on that one. I guess you win some and you lose some. Clemson ran out the clock a couple of minutes later and I signed off at the end of the game, never reporting Woody's fateful blow. Hayes was fired the next day.

"Our final stop at *The* Ohio State University shows us parts of the campus which, prior to the school's founding, were landmarks for a route on the Underground Railroad where enslaved African Americans escaping the South followed the Freedom Train north to liberation. A placard placed in Columbus describing the secret network reads, 'The Underground Railroad was neither underground nor a railroad, but a system of loosely connected safe havens where those escaping the brutal conditions of slavery were sheltered, fed, clothed, nursed, concealed, disguised and instructed during their journey to freedom. Although this movement was one of America's greatest social, moral and humanitarian endeavors, the details about it were often cloaked in secrecy to protect those involved from the retribution of civil law and slave catchers. Ohio's history has been permanently shaped by the thousands of runaway slaves passing through or finding permanent residence in this state.'"

"Great history lesson," says the Ghost.

Next up we go back to 1889 where it's high noon on April twenty-second and we are witnesses to a massive land rush in the center of the United States that erupts with a pistol shot. Approximately two million acres of some of the best unoccupied public land in the country is up for grabs and an estimated fifty thousand settlers have lined up to get their shares.

"If you're one of the early pioneers and promoters of making this land available for settlement, you're called a Boomer," says Jackson. "If you're one of the people who literally jump the gun to grab your stake in Mother Earth, you're called a Sooner. This rough and wild area became known as the Oklahoma Territory and was eventually merged with the nearby Indian Territory to become the state of Oklahoma in 1907. In 1890, seventeen years prior to statehood, the University of Oklahoma was founded.

"It's only fitting that the school adopted red as an official color because the name 'Oklahoma' is formed by combining two Native American Choctaw words, 'okla' and 'humma,' meaning red people."

"Oklahoma loves their football," says Red. "I remember in the early 1950s, the school president went to the state legislators to make an appeal for an increase in school funding. He told them, 'We want to build a university the football team will be proud of.'"

"OU is among the elite of college football due in large part to the success of Bud Wilkinson and Barry Switzer," says Jackson. "Wilkinson took over in 1947 and brought the school its first three national championships during a run of thirteen consecutive conference titles. He also led the Sooners to a forty-seven-game winning streak, the longest streak in college football history."

"Can you imagine playing the equivalent of four and a half seasons without losing a single game?" I ask.

"That's amazing," says Red. "It's hard enough to go undefeated in a single season."

"Nobody has come close to that record since," I add.

"Switzer matched Wilkinson's three national championships

along with twelve conference titles over his sixteen seasons," says Keith. "He's also one of those rare head coaches to win both a college football national championship and Super Bowl title in their careers joining Jimmy Johnson and Pete Carroll as the only three to accomplish that feat. Unfortunately, Switzer's time at Oklahoma ended in a barrage of off-field scandals resulting in his resignation in 1989."

From Norman, Oklahoma, we swoop into Bryant–Denny Stadium in Tuscaloosa to see the final seconds of an Alabama victory over Tennessee tick away. Right on cue, after victory is assured, the Tide's Million Dollar Band strikes up "The Hey Song" and the crowd launches into their traditional Rammer Jammer cheer shouting,

"Hey Vols!
Hey Vols!
Hey Vols!
We just beat the hell outta' you!
Rammer Jammer, Yellow Hammer
Give 'em hell, Alabama!"

They repeat it a couple more times for emphasis.

"The school used to do the cheer before games as well, replacing the lyrics 'We just' with 'We're gonna' but the administration decided it was a little over the top so they banned it," I explain. "They tried to get rid of it after victories as well, but the student body overwhelmingly voted to bring it back. As for 'The Hey Song,' its best days are behind it, especially in the sports world, since its creator Gary Glitter was convicted as a child sex offender in 2006."

"Prior to 1925," says Jackson, "Alabama hadn't earned much national recognition in football. Will Rogers referred to the Crimson Tide as the 'Tusca-losers.' Today, Alabama sits firmly entrenched among the sport's elite claiming eighteen national championships, seven more than any of the other Great Eight."

Touring the Alabama campus, it's impossible to miss the influence of Bear Bryant. Their stadium, a museum, multiple buildings and a street are named in his honor. His statue stands alongside their other national championship–winning football coaches.

"Paul Bryant earned his nickname for wrestling a captive bear at a carnival sideshow as a young teen," says Jackson. "His choice in hats inspired fans to adopt houndstooth as an unofficial school color. Bear led the Tide to six national championships and thirteen conference titles in his twenty-five years as head coach. The simple plow-hand from Arkansas retired with more wins than any other coach in major college history. Bear insisted that when he stopped coaching, he would die. True to his word, when he retired after his last game in 1982, he died a month later.

"Alabama has the enviable distinction of employing two

of the greatest head coaches in history. With the Tide's most recent national championship in 2020, Nick Saban surpassed Bryant by winning his seventh title and effectively ended any debate about who is the greatest coach of all time."

"There's no doubt in my mind he's at the top of the list," says Red.

"Saban's accomplishments are truly remarkable and he is still going strong, so his story continues to be written," I add. "It's always difficult to compare coaches from different eras, but as great as Bryant was, five of his titles were shared with other schools, whereas only one of Saban's titles was split with another school, USC in 2003. His other six were all won under a system that generated a unanimous decision."

"On the other hand," says Red, "Bear *was* able to win his first three titles hamstrung by segregation, when much of the country had already integrated their rosters."

"Yes, but Bryant had the advantage of coaching without any scholarship restrictions throughout the majority of his career," I counter. "Saban has worked under the eighty-five-scholarship limit essentially his entire head coaching tenure. When you consider how evolved and competitive the game is today, I think it's clear Saban will be remembered as the greatest of all time in college football."

• • •

The tour heads out west to USC where football alum Frank Gifford materializes to describe a school tradition. “One of the first things a new student learns when they set foot on the USC campus is how to greet a fellow Trojan,” says Frank. “They teach you to raise your hand with the two-finger victory salute and give a spirited ‘Fight On!’

“Here at SC, the greeting is an enthusiastic gesture of comradery; however, the origin of the victory sign has a grislier legend dating back over three thousand years when Trojan warriors would cut off the index and middle fingers of their defeated opponents’ right hands to prevent them from being able to wield a sword again in battle. The Trojans would then make the V gesture to mock their conquered, eight-fingered enemies.

“Every school has its share of diehard fans,” says Gifford, “but none are more dedicated than Giles Pellerin, who attended a national record seven hundred ninety-seven *consecutive* USC football games.”

“I didn’t miss a single game, home or away, in seventy-two years,” Giles recalls from his old seat in the Coliseum. “The streak began in 1925 while I was a student at SC and included games in seventy-five stadiums and more than fifty cities. There were several close calls of the streak being broken but somehow, I always managed to get to the games. That is until 1998, when I was at the Rose Bowl for the annual game against UCLA. I became seriously ill and told my brother we had to leave. I made it as far as the parking lot, where I died of cardiac arrest at the age of ninety-one. I never played the game, but I love it. There's just a certain spirit about college football."

"Both Howard Jones and John McKay share the spotlight as the greatest coaches in USC history," says Gifford. "Jones' Thundering Herd and McKay's Tailback U each produced four national championships. McKay was one of the most colorful coaches in the game and was known for his trademark sense of humor."

McKay shows up talking about a 51–0 loss to Notre Dame in 1966. "I told my team it doesn't matter," he says. "There are seven hundred fifty million people in China who don't even know this game was played. The next day, a guy called me from China and asked, 'What happened, Coach?'

"After another tough loss I had to explain to the press, 'We didn't tackle well today, but we made up for it by not blocking.' When a reporter asked about my team's execution I replied, 'I'm in favor of it.' One time, somebody asked me about the importance of playing with emotion. I told them, 'Emotion is highly overrated in football. My wife Corky is emotional as hell, but she can't play football worth a damn.'"

McKay disappears into the darkness and a moment later the silence is filled by the Michigan Marching Band playing "The Victors" as we jump to Ann Arbor. John Phillip Sousa, America's March King, whose band was the first to perform the song publicly, called it "the best college march ever written."

"When you look across the landscape of college football,"

says Keith Jackson, "it's easy to pick a Michigan football player out of a crowd thanks to his unmistakable blue-and-maize winged helmet. That's what head coach Fritz Crisler had in mind when he brought the helmet design with him from Princeton in 1938."

"Our plain black leather helmets weren't flashy enough for me," says Crisler. "I wanted to add some style to the helmet and make it easier for my passers to spot our receivers downfield, so I ordered our helmets to be colored blue with the bright maize-color wing design in front and stripes along the top. The design was patterned after the shape of the protective leather padding that was found on many types of helmets manufactured during that era."

"When a school has won more games than any other program in the history of college football and you combine that with eleven national championships and forty-two conference titles, it's a foregone conclusion that the University of Michigan is one of the all-time greats," says Jackson.

"You can't help but point out that a large chunk of their national success is completely skewed toward the first half of the twentieth century," says Red. "Of Michigan's eleven national titles, ten of them were won before 1949. In more than seventy years since, they have one lone championship, in 1997."

"You can bet everyone connected with the school desperately wants to change that," I say.

"The Fighting Irish owe a debt of gratitude to Michigan for

helping Notre Dame get their football program off the ground in 1887," says Jackson. "The Wolverines agreed to travel to South Bend that year to play the Irish in the school's first game. Michigan had the benefit of an eight-year head start playing football and Notre Dame's team was just being organized, so the Wolverines started out the day by conducting an instructional scrimmage for the Irish players before the actual game was played, which Michigan won 8–0.

"Fielding Yost is responsible for the greatest run of success in Michigan history, leading the Wolverines to six national championships and ten conference titles over his twenty-five years in charge."

"In my first year in 1901," says Yost, "we went undefeated and won the school's first national championship. We outscored our opponents 555–0 that year. They invited us out to Pasadena to play Stanford in what turned out to be the first Rose Bowl game ever played. We were beating them so soundly that with about eight minutes left to play, Stanford raised the white flag and asked for the game to be called with the score at 49–0. The game was so lopsided that the Tournament of Roses dropped football from their event schedule for the next thirteen years."

"Any discussion about Michigan football has to include an honorable mention for Bo Schembechler," says Jackson. "Bo led the Wolverines for twenty-one seasons and won more games and conference titles than any other coach in school history. But he never won a national championship, which was his most sought-after achievement, that is of course, after beating Ohio State."

Leaving Michigan, Red and I zoom into Cornhusker country where we are swallowed up by a sellout crowd of over 90,000 fans known as The Sea of Red.

"Nebraska is on an all-time record sellout streak of three hundred seventy-five consecutive home games that started back in 1962," says Keith. "The streak is so old it's estimated that only eight percent of the nation's current population was even alive when it started. A Cornhusker home game is a major event where Memorial Stadium could qualify as the third-largest city in the state on game days."

"Husker fans are widely known as a class act," says Red. "Win or lose, The Sea of Red will stand and applaud the visiting team for putting on a good show as they leave the field. The school honors them with the following inscription displayed over every stadium entrance: THROUGH THESE GATES PASS THE GREATEST FANS IN COLLEGE FOOTBALL."

"Prior to the 1960s," says Keith, "NU's football program had limited success. In its early years, the team was called the Bugeaters, named after the insect-eating bats that are common to the Nebraska plains. Even when they got a new nickname, it wasn't until 1941 that the Cornhuskers played in their first bowl game. Bob Devaney took over the program in 1962 and quickly turned Nebraska into a force in the Big Eight Conference. In 1969 he promoted long-time assistant Tom Osborne to offensive coordinator. Osborne retooled the Husker offense and kick-started a new era of Nebraska football. During Devaney's eleven years as head coach, he led the Huskers to back-to-back national titles in 1970 and 1971 and eight conference titles. He stepped down after the 1972 season to focus on his athletic director duties and elevated Osborne to run the football program.

"As head coach, Tom Osborne established an unprecedented model of excellence at Nebraska, leading the program for the next twenty-five years. Between 1993 and 1997 he produced one of the most dominant runs in college football history, compiling a 60-3 record and winning three national championships in four years. He won thirteen conference titles and his teams went to twenty-five consecutive bowl games."

"Osborne also suffered his share of near misses, losing the Orange Bowl three times with the national title on the line in 1982, 1984 and 1994. He set the bar so high, he confessed that one of his biggest challenges as head coach was convincing the people of Nebraska that a 10-1record is not a losing season.

"The final leg of our tour takes us down to the Lone Star State. Although the Texas Longhorns may not claim as many national championships as some of their fellow blue bloods, they certainly are excelling in an especially important category—money. According to a recent survey published in the *Wall Street Journal*, the Longhorns football program is valued at $1.24 billion. That's a lot of black gold. The valuation is based on analysis of what a football program might be worth if it could be sold like an NFL team considering the program's revenue, expenses and growth projections. At UT they know how to monetize football. By golly, the school even has its own TV network.

"The Texas coaching honor roll is headed by Darrell Royal, who stands at the head of the class in school history by winning three of the school's four national championships. In his entire twenty-three-year career as a head coach at three different schools, Darrell Royal never had a losing season. He spent twenty years at Texas and was named national coach of the year five times. Like Woody Hayes, Royal hated the forward pass and believed in a strong running game. He also understood the importance of what we now call the 'red zone' decades before the term became part of the sport's vernacular."

Royal appears in the locker room talking to his team. "Boys," he says, "football games are decided from the twenty-yard line on in. All that other running and panting out in the middle of the field is just entertaining spectators and wearing out grass. And by the way, you've got to think lucky. If you fall into a mud hole, check your back pocket. You just might have caught a fish."

"Royal is credited with introducing the wishbone offense to major college football," says Jackson. "The wishbone, or triple-option, was the most productive and innovative offensive scheme of the 1970s and '80s. It was developed by Emory Bellard, one of Royal's assistant coaches, who came up with the scheme as a successful high school coach before coming to UT."

The tour takes us on a pregame fly-over of the stadium named in Royal's honor as a capacity crowd, in burnt orange, sings "The Eyes of Texas" while flashing the Hook 'em Horns hand signal inspired by the school's Longhorn mascot.

"When you have a huge, powerful animal with horns like Bevo as your mascot," says Keith, "you're probably wondering how you keep him from running wild and wreaking havoc. The answer is pretty simple; he's a steer, not a bull, so he's pretty docile."

"You probably would be too if you had your testicles removed," jokes Red.

"Ha. Shut up!" I say, elbowing him in the ribs.

"I heard there was a time when the student body was concerned about Bevo's masculinity," Red says. "They were even considering equipping him with prosthetic testicles."

"What will they think of next?" I wonder aloud.

We fall into darkness again as the tour comes to an end. A constellation of brightly colored logos forms overhead: Alabama, Notre Dame, Ohio State, Oklahoma, USC, Michigan, Nebraska and Texas.

"Whoa, Nellie! There you have it, the All-Time Great Eight of College Football. This is Keith Jackson signing off."

The lights come on and we return to the main hall.

"That was phenomenal, pal," says Red. "You could sell tickets to that."

"If only we had a need for money. I'm glad you liked it. Ready to get back to work?"

"Wait, now it's my turn," he says. "I'd like to show you something. Are you game?"

"Absolutely!"

Snap!

16

Homecoming

We're standing in the center of Wheaton, Illinois, the Ghost's boyhood hometown, which sits about thirty miles due west of Chicago.

"Boy have things changed around here," says Red. "I moved here with my family in 1908 when I was five years old and Wheaton was a small town of about four thousand people. Now it's over fifty thousand."

"That's a different world than what I'm used to," I say. "My high school had more kids in it than the entire population of Wheaton back then."

"Dad rented a house when we first arrived," Red says, "but he couldn't make enough to cover the expenses so after a while, we moved in with my Uncle Luther to cut costs. We had a pretty nomadic existence moving around town several times over the years.

"When I was in the eighth grade, I lived on my Uncle Ernest's farm. I'd wake up at five o'clock every morning to feed the horses and milk the cows before breakfast. Then I'd hitch the horses up to the wagon and take the milk into the local dairy. I'd get back home and ride my bike to school. At the end of the day I would have to clean out the barn, feed the horses and milk the cows again. It was a lot of work, so after about a year I'd had enough and moved back in with my father and brother Garland. We lived in an apartment over a store right here on Front Street."

We stroll to the edge of town and Red points out an area that used to be a vacant lot where he played football as a kid. "There was a big crest in the middle of the field that divided it in half with about fifty yards on each side. The other team would line up to kick off to us and we couldn't even see them on the other side of the hill. The ball would come flying our way and then the other team would appear over the crest, stampeding toward us. We had a great time. I was always playing against older kids and used to take a beating, but it toughened me up."

"My favorite place to play as a kid was a vacant lot at the end of our block," I say. "We used to call it the dump because it was the neighborhood junkyard. Anything too big to stuff into a garbage can would find its way there on a regular basis. There'd be worn-out tires, mattresses, couches, appliances, and rolls of carpet; we'd invent new games to play with whatever was lying around. There was an abandoned pickup covered with graffiti stashed in the far corner. It had been picked clean by the neighborhood, but the steering wheel was still there and my friends and I would sit on boxes in the cab and drive wherever our imaginations would take us. We had our own living room arrangement set up close by with a beat-up sofa, a three-legged coffee table propped up by a milk crate, filthy orange shag carpeting and a TV set with the screen kicked in. We'd sit back and watch the gangbangers cruise by and hope we wouldn't catch a stray bullet."

"Wheaton wasn't quite as exciting as Los Angeles," Red jokes, "but I loved the place. It was a great spot for a kid to grow up. It instilled midwestern values and sensibilities in us. The highlight of my days as a kid was playing football, baseball and basketball after school with my pals. During the summers, we used to ride our bikes every day for hours all over town.

"When I was eight years old, the doctors found that I had a heart murmur and immediately put the kibosh on any strenuous physical activity."

"I didn't know you had heart trouble," I say.

"Yeah, but I wasn't about to let it slow me down. I guess I was too young to understand how serious it could be; I used to have to sneak out to play ball. Fortunately, when I entered high school, I had a physical examination and the heart murmur had disappeared, so I was cleared to play sports.

"Wheaton High was an old, three-story brick building; it's long gone now. They ended up moving the school to a new location a few years after I graduated. We had one male teacher and, since he knew a little about sports, he became the coach of all our athletic teams. However, Wheaton High didn't have any athletic facilities, so we made do with what was available. Football was played on a grass field next to an apple orchard about a mile and a half away. Before we could play our games there, we had to clear the field of all the apples on the ground. We used vacant lots around town to serve as baseball fields and basketball was played in the gym at Wheaton College, where we also used their track for meets."

Red shows me the house he bought for his father in 1926. "I bought this house for twenty-five-thousand dollars, right after my first year in the pros. We put a lot of work into remodeling it and I had the place completely furnished by one of the big department stores in Chicago. Between my father, brother and I we had four cars, so we built a large, four-car garage on the lot next door and equipped it with everything you'd need for a first-class repair shop, including a grease pit and gasoline pump. I used to love working on the family cars."

The house is vacant with a For Sale sign out front. "This sure brings back memories," he says, as we wander around inside. "Dad really loved this house. We had always been so broke; it was one of the happiest days of my life when I gave him the keys to his own home."

Climbing the stairs up to the third floor, Red describes the den that used to be there. "This was one of Dad's favorite places—his man cave. It had wood-paneled walls, leather sofa and chairs, a pool table, poker table and a bar. As I told you a while back, this is where I got the idea for the Grotto. All of his cronies would regularly gather here. He had one of those old Philco radios that was as big as a television set and we'd sit around listening to the championship fights and big games."

We continue to walk around the neighborhood and Red recalls his days working on the ice truck. "Delivering ice was hard work. I had to walk miles every day going door to door, up and down stairs, carrying heavy blocks of ice. The job had its hazards as well; I used to get stabbed with ice picks, stuck with ice tongs, and drop ice blocks on my hands, feet and toes. My whole body would be sore from hauling seventy-five-pound blocks on my shoulders all day long. I did get seriously hurt one time at work. I had a habit of jumping on the running board of the truck while it was moving down the street in between deliveries. One summer morning, between my sophomore and junior year in high school, we were out on our route. The truck was rolling down the street, fully loaded with about three tons of ice, and as I jumped on the running board, I grabbed the handle on the side of the cab. The handle broke off in my hand and I fell under the truck. The back wheel ran over my left leg just above the knee. The pain was excruciating, and I went into shock."

"What happened from there?" I ask.

"Herman, the truck driver, got me to a doctor's office. The folks there worried my knee had been crushed and my leg might need to be amputated. The doctor said if the wheel had gone just an inch or two lower on my leg it could have been catastrophic. Even though my leg was saved, they only gave me a fifty-fifty chance of a full recovery. I was bedridden for about a month with my leg uncomfortably hung up in a sling. I was agonizing the entire time over whether I'd be able to make a full comeback. When I was growing up, all I ever wanted to be was a great athlete. Luckily, a couple of weeks after I could get out of bed, I was able to start walking again without much trouble. Eventually, I fully recovered and was able to play football that fall."

We walk over to the high school football field that is named in his honor. "In high school, I played football every fall, basketball every winter, and each spring I played baseball and ran track. I earned sixteen varsity letters along the way. People said I was the most publicized high school athlete in the state of Illinois."

"How did you do as a student?" I ask.

"Other than sports," he says, "school wasn't of much interest to me. I studied mainly just so I could maintain my eligibility. Near the end of my senior year, some recruiters from Michigan came down to see me. They made a great pitch to get me to come to their school. Since there were no athletic scholarships back then and everyone had to pay their own way, Michigan wasn't an option for me because I couldn't afford the tuition and expense of going to an out-of-state school."

"How did you end up at Illinois?"

"Since I was a resident of the state, the University of Illinois was the most affordable option for me. Bob Zuppke, the coach, didn't put much effort into recruiting. He thought it was beneath someone of his stature. His only pitch to get me to come to Illinois was during the state high school track championships in

Champaign my senior year. He was a nice enough guy and he came over to say hello. I remember him saying, 'If you come down here to school, I believe you'll stand a good chance of making our football team.' That was the extent of his recruiting pitch. Coach Zuppke and the school had a great reputation so that's how I became a Fighting Illini." Red pauses for a moment. "Why don't we head over to the campus," he says, snapping his fingers.

In a blink, we are surprised to find ourselves standing in a McDonald's parking lot.

"What are we doing here?" I ask.

"I have no idea. We're supposed to be in the middle of U of I."

Looking around, we have no clue where we are. We turn to each other shrugging our shoulders. "You always handle the navigation," I say. "What happened?"

"My GPS must be off," he says, scratching his head.

"You use GPS?" I ask.

"That's what I call it—the Ghost Positioning System. Heck, I don't know what it is. We just decide where we want to go and, in a snap, that's where we end up."

"Jessica, we need your help," he calls out. "Where are we?"

"I think you got your wires crossed, Red," Jessica says. "You're in Peoria."

"I must be getting too old for this; we need to be in Champaign. Can you get us over to U of I?"

"Sure, hold on," she says, and a second later we're standing outside of Illinois' Memorial Stadium in front of a massive bronze statue of the Ghost captured in a classic pose of him running with the ball.

"I was at the dedication ceremony for that statue in 2009," he says. "The Chancellor said he could feel I was here in spirit that day and he was right. I really appreciate everything the school did for me."

"That's a magnificent statue; you should be very proud," I say.

"They say it's about twelve feet tall and weighs over two thousand pounds."

The plaque in front of the statue reads:

Harold "Red" Grange
The Galloping Ghost
77

Red Grange is considered to be the greatest player in college football history. He lettered as a halfback from 1923 to '25, earning All-America honors all three seasons. His most memorable performance occurred in the Memorial Stadium dedication game against Michigan on October 18, 1924, when he scored four touchdowns the first four times he touched the ball, on runs of 95, 67, 56 and 44 yards. He was inducted as a charter member into both the College and Pro Football Halls of Fame.

A streak of fire, a breath of flame; Eluding all who reach and clutch;

A gray ghost thrown into the game; That rival hands may never touch;

A rubber bounding, blasting soul, whose destination is the goal —Red Grange of Illinois!

Grantland Rice, legendary sportswriter

The statue overlooks Grange Grove, which is a large, grassy tailgate area just outside the stadium. "There used to be a parking lot here, and a few years ago they converted it into this great gathering spot," he says. "On game days, the place is filled with fans who cheer on the team as they walk through the middle of the grove, led by the Marching Illini drumline and cheerleaders on their way into the stadium."

We go inside to look at the field and have a seat in the front row. It's a calm, sun-filled day and there isn't a living soul around the place. As we sit there in silence for several minutes, I can imagine Red is strolling down memory lane. His name and number are emblazoned at the top of the press box along with Dick Butkus, the former Illinois and Chicago Bears great. Red says he and Butkus are the only two football players in school history to have their numbers retired.

"How did you end up with your famous number seventy-seven?" I ask.

"When I was a freshman, I was standing in line as they were

passing out uniforms," he says. "The guy in front of me got number seventy-six and the guy behind me got seventy-eight. I never asked for that number; it was just given to me. After my first year, I felt it was kind of lucky, so I stuck with it. The school retired it after my last game in 1925.

"It's funny. When I started school here, I didn't even plan on going out for football. I always felt basketball was my best sport, so I was going to do that as well as play baseball. However, I pledged the Zeta Psi fraternity when I first got on campus, and they lined us all up and told us what school activities they wanted us to pursue. They knew I was a pretty good football player in high school, so they wanted me to go out for the team. I told them I thought I was too small for football, weighing only one hundred sixty-six pounds, but they had their minds made up. Football carried more prestige than other sports on campus, which would reflect better on the fraternity, so football it was. I went to practice the first day and there were well over a hundred guys going out for the freshman team. Every one of them looked bigger than me and it seemed useless to stick around. I went back to the fraternity house and explained that I didn't have any chance against all those other bigger guys. They proceeded to get a paddle off the wall and made me bend over and grab my ankles. I decided right then I didn't need any more convincing, so I agreed to give football another shot. I showed up at practice the next day and began to realize that even though most of the guys out there were bigger than I was, they weren't as fast, and they couldn't handle a football as well as I could. By the end of the first week, the number of players remaining had dropped significantly and I had earned a starting position at halfback. They eventually named me captain of the team.

"We used to scrimmage the varsity a couple of times each week. We lost the first one by two points but after that we got the better of them most of the time by wide margins. Turns out our freshman team was one of the best the school ever had, and Coach Zuppke got so wrapped up in what we meant for the future, he spent more time with us than his own varsity. I wish freshmen could have been eligible to play varsity back then; I would love to have played varsity for four years. The core of that freshman team was a big reason Illinois went undefeated and won the national championship the following year, in 1923."

"Did you go out for basketball while you were here?"

"No, but I did play some baseball. It's interesting how things work out sometimes. If I hadn't been forced to play football by my fraternity, I don't know if I would have ever played the game again after high school."

"What's your favorite memory of playing here?" I ask.

"It has to be the Michigan game in 1924. Just the buildup to it was incredible. It actually started the season before, when I was a sophomore. Both Illinois and Michigan were undefeated, and we shared the conference and national champion titles. Due to a scheduling quirk, we didn't play Michigan that year and there was always a debate about who was the better team. It would be decided on the field the next year on October eighteenth right here at Memorial Stadium. It was Homecoming Week and they were also dedicating the new stadium that day. There were over sixty-seven thousand people here and I heard several thousand more were turned away.

"Michigan felt they would beat us handily and made it known publicly. Fielding Yost was saying, 'All Grange can do is run' and he was going to have all eleven Michigan defenders focused on stopping me whenever I had the ball. He said, 'We'll let the other fellow rush the ball and waste his energy in his own territory. We believe that position is more important than possession. Football games aren't won—they're lost.'

"Coach Zuppke helped fan the flames by sending us all letters during the summer telling us how Michigan was expecting to pummel us. By the time we returned to school in the fall and reported for training camp, we were so fired up about beating Michigan that it became our top priority."

"Coming into the game," I recall, "Michigan hadn't lost in almost three years and had given up only four touchdowns in the previous two seasons combined. They were one of the great dynasties in the country."

"Yep, Yost had built the Michigan program into a national power and even though he was the school's athletic director at the time, he was still running the football team through a figurehead coach named George Little. But Yost had met his match in Bob Zuppke. They had an unusual relationship; they were great pals but they detested each other. Yost was Zuppke's most hated rival. Zuppke, however, was one of the game's great strategists. He always seemed to come up with a brilliant plan, especially for big games.

"For example, after pregame warm-ups that day, our team gathered in the locker room and Zuppke came up with a strange idea. He said, 'It's quite hot outside. I want you all to take your socks off. You'll feel better and cooler without those heavy socks.' It turned out to be a great psychological ploy because, when we came out onto the field prior to kickoff, Yost and his Michigan team were suspicious of what they saw and thought there had to be some sort of trick. They thought we had greased our legs to be able to slip tackles. At the very least, they thought not wearing socks had to be against the rules. Michigan protested to the officials who said there was nothing they could do. Their coach and team captain checked our legs to make sure there was no foreign substance on them. Only then were they satisfied and finally agreed to start the game. The stunt worked, however, and threw Michigan off balance. They were clearly distracted."

Red continues to detail Zuppke's game strategies and other recollections. After several minutes he hops out of his seat and walks down to the field. He begins to jog around as if retracing some of his former runs. The Ghost has returned to his hallowed stomping grounds. Red goes down to the far goal line and turns around facing the field. He appears to be waiting for something, like a kickoff. As I watch him my eyes start to play tricks on me. His image distorts like a TV picture with bad reception. Is it the glare from the sun? It's like he's transforming.

Gradually, he comes back into focus. To my surprise, the Ghost has turned back the clock to reclaim his prime as the twenty-one-year-old All-American halfback. Standing on the goal line in full uniform, he stares anxiously into the stands as if looking for someone. The silence of the vacant stadium is broken by the growing rumble of a standing-room-only crowd that materializes as the structure morphs back to its original state. The weather warms to a more summer-like baseball day rather than a fall football Saturday. Players, coaches and referees spill out onto the gridiron, which is manicured to perfection. I notice a game program lying on a seat; the cover reads "Illinois vs. Michigan, October 18, 1924."

This is *the* game! I'm about to witness history as it happened, sixty-seven years before I was born, a game considered by many to be one of the greatest performances of all time in college sports. Somehow, Red has been able to bend time to relive this moment. Today, the Galloping Ghost is born. I settle in to watch my famous friend.

Michigan's squad lines up to kick off and the ball sails deep into Illinois' territory. Red makes the catch at his own five-yard line and takes off like a flash, straight down the center of the field. A gang of Michigan defenders is closing in on him when he sticks his foot in the ground to cut right and accelerates around them. He makes another quick cutback to the left and races up the opposite sideline toward Michigan's goal line with one man to beat. The Wolverine tackler takes a desperate leap at the Ghost and comes up empty as Grange goes in for the score. The Ghost's speed and elusiveness is stunning. The sockless Illini have stolen a page from Michigan's playbook—score first and score fast before your opponent knows what hit them.

I remember seeing some clips of this game from the newsreel Jessica put me through, but being in the grainy, two-dimensional, black-and-white film doesn't come close to the experience of being here, seeing the action firsthand, where I'm able to fully appreciate Red's unique ability to make cuts and change speeds in the blink of an eye.

Michigan insists on kicking off after Illinois' score rather than receive and get possession of the ball. This time Red catches the ball deep again and is stopped at his own twenty-yard line. After a couple of changes in possession, Illinois gets the ball back and, on second down, Red takes the handoff at his thirty-three-yard line. He sprints around left end, then cuts back to his right to pick up his blockers and he is gone, sixty-seven yards for his second score. After crossing the goal line, in a move reminiscent of the rule in earlier days of the game, he touches the ball down in the end zone.

Three possessions later, Illinois has the ball at its own forty-four. They hand off to the Ghost, who takes off around right end. He cuts back to the center of the field and makes a dash for the end zone with nothing but green grass in front of him—fifty-six yards and his third touchdown. When Red gets to the open field, he is able to accelerate to another gear that others simply cannot match.

Not only is Michigan unprepared to handle Red's speed, but their scouting reports said nothing about his ability to make these deadly cutbacks against the grain. Although Red was an open-field runner, his tendencies were to take the ball outside around either of the ends and let his speed take over on the straightaways. The cutbacks or S-shaped runs were part of Zuppke's brilliant game plan for Michigan. The Wolverines were coached to follow Grange to whatever side he was initially headed and then load up to stop him along the sideline. But Zuppke had the Ghost and his blockers trained to run the S curve, which worked to perfection repeatedly against the Wolverines.

Coach Zuppke is sitting in his chair on the sideline smoking a cigar, watching his plan unfold. Since coaching from the sidelines was prohibited in those days, there wasn't much else he could do but sit back and watch. He had put his plan in place during the week leading up to the game and he had to rely on his players to call their own plays and execute the strategy. The same eleven players go both ways, so you only have the few minutes during halftime to revise your game plan. Michigan had no answers to stop the bleeding.

Minutes later Red gets another opportunity and doesn't disappoint. He takes the ball at Michigan's forty-four yard line and heads around right end. Just like his previous score, he draws the Wolverines' secondary over toward the sideline and makes a sharp cutback to the left. He avoids a couple of tacklers and takes it all the way home. The excitement in the stadium is fever-pitched. The Michigan players, like their fans, are in shock. Red is single-handedly dismantling one of the greatest teams in America.

With Michigan's incoherence on full display, they kick off to Illinois again for the fourth straight time. At this point you can tell that Red is completely gassed. He has played every down on both offense and defense and has run for over three hundred yards and scored four touchdowns. All that, and there's still three minutes left in the first quarter. Illinois calls a timeout and the Ghost jogs to the sideline for a well-deserved rest. The crowd is in an absolute frenzy with a standing ovation that seems to go on forever. Many in attendance thought they were watching one of the best games of the year; little did they know they were witnessing one of the greatest performances in American football history.

As Red comes to the sideline, Zuppke doesn't congratulate him. "With any brains, you could have had *five* touchdowns if you had timed your cut better on that earlier run," he jokingly berates him. Zuppke isn't about to let Grange get a big head.

The Ghost is done for the first half; the rules won't allow

him to return until after halftime. The teams go into the locker room at the break with Illinois leading 27–7. When Red returns in the third quarter, he notches his fifth rushing touchdown from twelve yards out. He puts a capper on the day when he throws for a sixth touchdown in the final quarter to give Illinois an insurmountable lead. The Wolverines score a meaningless touchdown in the fourth quarter and the game ends—Illinois 39 and Michigan 14.

Memorial Stadium is a madhouse of excitement. Red congratulates his teammates and pauses a few moments on the field to soak in the atmosphere. While standing amidst the thunderous cheers, everyone in attendance that day—the players, coaches, referees, vendors, reporters, ushers and fans—begins to vanish. The stadium slowly transforms back to its present-day state and is once again silently vacant. The Ghost is standing alone in the middle of the field and I walk out to congratulate him. As I get closer, I can see he is a bundle of exhaustion and elation. He is wearing the effects of having played a violent, physical game. Blood is running down from a cut on the bridge of his nose; bruises, dirt and sweat mark his face, but today it's the look of a true champion. Seeing the twenty-one-year-old phenom in his prime, up close, helps somewhat explain how he can do what he does on a football field. He is a solid rock of muscle, tough as nails and gifted with exceptional speed, agility and elusiveness.

"That was incredible, Red," I congratulate him with a

handshake and a hug. "The greatest players deliver their best performances in the biggest games."

"Thanks, pal," he replies. "We had a score to settle with Michigan that day. We were determined to prove we were the better team. Zuppke's cutback strategy was the key to the game. I just played the only way I knew how. When you have the football and eleven guys are after you, if you're smart, you'll run. It was no big deal; my grandmother could have scored touchdowns that day and she was ninety years old. Our blocking and execution were that good."

"I kept track of your stats. You had a total of four hundred two yards: two hundred twelve rushing, one hundred twenty-six on kick returns, and sixty-four yards passing, not to mention the six touchdowns—five on the ground and the one you threw for a sixth."

"Contrary to what the plaque in front of my statue outside says, I didn't score the first four times I touched the ball. There were a couple of kick returns and carries where I was stopped, in between the first four touchdowns."

"Don't worry, pal, I won't hold it against you," I joke. "So, Warren Brown of the *Chicago Herald-Examiner* gave you the Galloping Ghost nickname after that game. Lots of people think it was Grantland Rice."

"Yeah, although Rice often gets credit for it, he wasn't even here that day. He was at the Polo Grounds in New York that Saturday covering the Notre Dame versus Army game. That was the day he gave the 'Four Horsemen' nickname to the Notre Dame backfield. Warren Brown is the same fellow that nicknamed Babe Ruth 'The Sultan of Swat.'"

We turn to walk toward the exit and I mention, "Just before kickoff you were looking around at the stands. What were you looking for?"

"I couldn't remember where the people from Wheaton were sitting that day," he replies. "We had about seventy-five hundred people from town at the game. My dad was there, as he usually was. It felt great when I spotted him and the whole group."

"It's too bad you couldn't talk to him after the game before everyone vanished."

"No, I never got a chance to see him after the game that day. It was bedlam everywhere, in the locker room and back at the fraternity house."

"Why couldn't you have tried to see him just now?"

"It didn't happen that day so it couldn't happen today. Everything needs to play out just as it did back then. It's one of the rules about going back like that."

I glance over at the Ghost and he has returned to his eighty-seven-year-old self in his familiar street clothes. "Why did you change back?"

"It was wonderful to relive that game and be twenty-one again, but this is who I am now. I lived a long life. I'm sorry yours got cut short. You had a lot of living ahead of you."

“You know what, I wouldn’t have traded the chance to meet you and be on this journey for anything else in the world. How about we get back to camp.”

Snap!

• • •

“Welcome back, gentlemen,” says Belvedere, greeting us at the office door. “By the way, there’s someone inside that wishes to see you, Mr. Kyle.”

“Thanks, Belvedere.” We enter the room and I see the image of someone with their back turned gazing out the window surrounded by sunlight. As I approach, even from behind, I recognize the unmistakable outline of the visitor and my heart jumps into my throat.

“Dad?”

“Hello, son.”

17
Reunited

A chill runs down my spine as I move to embrace my father. It's been sixteen years since he took his life and the horrific vision of that final day is seared into my memory. I feel a surge of anger emerge, but it is quickly overtaken by the intense joy and surprise at being able to see him once again. We are two fully grown men, close enough in age now to be brothers, locked in a clinch neither wants to break.

"You look good, son," he says, as we pull back from each other, our eyes red, soaked with tears. "You grew up to become an outstanding young man. I can't tell you how grateful I am to see you again."

I'm choked by a jumble of emotions and strain to find the words to respond. I snap out of it long enough to make a simple introduction. "Dad, I'd like you to meet my good friend, Red Grange."

"Eric McGinnis," he says, extending his hand. "It's truly an honor to meet you, Mr. Grange. Jessica told me you've been a tremendous friend to my son. I can't thank you enough."

"Please, call me Red. You have a remarkable son, Eric. I'm proud to call him my friend."

An awkward pause hangs in the air as everyone seems unsure

of what to say. Red wisely decides to excuse himself. "I'm gonna leave you fellas to catch up," he says, turning toward the door. He motions for me to join him in the hallway.

"I'm sorry to spring this on you, pal," he whispers. "I had Jessica do some checking and she was able to locate him. I thought about telling you we were trying to find him, but I felt it was best this way. She said he's not doing well and can really use your help; you need to square things with him. I hope you guys can work it out. Good luck!"

I return to the office and lock eyes with my father in silence. "Let's have a seat," I finally say, but when I start to continue, he interrupts.

"Wait a minute, Kyle. I have something I want to say. What I did was terrible. Ever since that day, not a moment has gone by that I haven't been punished with sorrow and guilt for leaving you and Mom that way and putting you both through that anguish. I have always prayed for the opportunity to see you again and try to explain so that you might be able to understand. I've been locked away in purgatory ever since I died, hoping for some kind of redemption. Jessica found me and said she knew where you were. Now my prayers have been answered."

"All this time, I've never been able to forgive you," I confess. "It has eaten away at me for years. My anger toward you is compounded by the disappointment I have in myself for not letting go and finding a way to forgive. I loved you so much and always looked up to you for strength and courage. You were my hero and then you were gone. I guess I expected too much from you and couldn't believe you would give up on yourself and leave Mom and me behind.

"Killing yourself forced us into really tough times. You didn't leave any money or insurance for us. Mom was working two jobs. I virtually dropped out, started ditching school, and gave up on sports and my dreams. I almost got sucked into gang life. You absolutely let me down; I had to grow up really fast and I hated you for the longest time."

"You have every right to feel the way you do," he replies. "I made a horrible mistake and have been paying for it ever since. You and Mom were the bright spots in my life, but otherwise, things were very dark for me. The war took an awful toll and I just couldn't deal with it anymore. When I got back from the Gulf, I lived every day trying to crowd out the memories of the terrible things we endured over there.

"What were you going through?" I ask.

"The nights were the worst; I used to dread going to bed every night. I'd just lie awake tossing and turning, so I started drinking to try to knock myself out. When I did fall asleep, the nightmares would come. They haunted me with a vicious grip that wouldn't let go. Your mom saw that they were getting worse. I'd be asleep thrashing around in bed, drenched in sweat, and wake up screaming. It was really scaring her."

After a lengthy silence, appearing reluctant to relive the memories, he explains, "A lot of people back in the U.S.

thought of the Gulf War and Desert Storm as some kind of video game with surgical airstrikes of precision bombing. Many of the images fed to the public were taken from bombers at altitudes that erased the human presence on the ground. But the things we endured in combat were horrific.

"Our barracks in Saudi Arabia were bombed by a Scud missile. The aftermath was gruesome: twenty-eight men killed, another forty-eight injured. Bodies were ripped apart, blood everywhere, men with limbs torn off. One Marine was decapitated by shrapnel. His head was nowhere to be found. Amazingly, I came out of it unharmed.

"A good friend of mine was fighting in Kuwait. He and six other Marines were in an armored vehicle that was destroyed by a missile. It was fired from a U.S. Air Force A-10 jet. They called it fratricide—friendly fire.

"On the final day of the war, Iraqi military were retreating from Kuwait after their invasion. We had them pinned down on a highway. Our jets had bombed both ends of a four-mile stretch of road, trapping hundreds of their tanks, armored cars, and trucks in a massive traffic jam alongside civilian vehicles. For nearly ten hours, our planes strafed the area again and again, obliterating every vehicle on that road, roughly two thousand in total. It was a massive turkey shoot that became known as the Highway of Death.

"When the air siege had stopped, they had us move into the area on foot. The carnage and destruction we saw on the ground was unimaginable. Although many of the vehicles' occupants had escaped on foot through the desert when the bombing started, hundreds of others weren't so lucky. We came across a burned-out Iraqi transport; charred bodies lying in the sand were scattered all around the vehicle. One soldier remaining in the truck appeared to have been trapped in the driver's seat. The windshield was missing, and it looked as though he was fighting to save his life by trying to climb out over the dashboard when he was consumed by the flames. I'll never forget the carbonized remains of his tortured face glaring out from the vehicle.

"I've relived the horrors of that war constantly from that moment on. I became an alcoholic and drank more and more but it wouldn't kill the pain or stop the nightmares."

"Did you try to get some help?" I ask.

"I went to counseling; they said I had post-traumatic stress disorder, but the sessions were more than I could handle. They wanted me to open those wounds and talk about it again and again. I couldn't bring myself to follow through; that was a big mistake. I thought I could deal with it by myself and the problem would go away over time, but it kept getting worse. The booze took over my life, clouded my mind, and drove me to suicide."

"I should have known how much trouble you were having when I came into the kitchen that night and you had the gun on the table," I say regretfully.

"You can't put any blame on yourself, Kyle; you were only ten years old. Besides, you probably saved my life that night. I was in bad shape and was seriously considering putting the gun in my mouth and pulling the trigger. If you hadn't come in, I probably would have followed through with it.

"I was drunk the afternoon I went into the garage; everything appeared so hopeless. Suicide offered an escape; I was worn down and could finally have some peace. It was the worst decision I could have made, and I've regretted it with all my heart ever since," he says, breaking down, his head in his hands.

I can't hold back the tears and move to his side. "I'm sorry, Dad," I say, hugging him just like that little ten-year-old kid in our kitchen so many years ago.

"Me too, son," he sighs. "Me too."

18
Snap

Being able to reunite with my dad and reconcile my feelings for him is one of the greatest gifts I could ever imagine. An enormous weight has been lifted now that I'm finally able to let go of the toxic emotions I've kept buried for so long.

"I'm so thankful to have this second chance with you, son," he says. "It's a tremendous relief to be able to express my sorrow for what happened and explain what I was going through."

"It was all Red's idea," I disclose. "He's the one who asked Jessica to find you and bring us together."

"I still can't get over it," he says, shaking his head. "We're here with Red Grange—the Galloping Ghost. It sounds like you guys have had an incredible time. Jessica told me about some of your exploits."

"He's a great guy, Dad. You'll really like him," I say admiringly. "Hey, let's take a walk. I'd like to show you around the camp."

• • •

While roaming around the facility I show him the work that's being done in the research lab by Dr. Charcot and his team. We stop by Red's Gridiron so he can experience the controlled pandemonium inside the massive sports bar and then contrast that with the solitary confinement of the Ivory Tower. We finish off with the tour of The Great Eight. All along the way, I'm able to catch him up on the details of my life since he died.

"It was awful not being part of your life all those years," Dad says. "Until Jessica found me, I had been completely isolated, trapped in a dismal no-man's land. You've had a challenging journey; I couldn't be prouder of the man you've become. It's amazing what you're doing here at the camp."

Upon returning to the office, we find Red and Belvedere in a misty-eyed hug, patting each other on the back. "What is going on around here?" I ask facetiously. "All of a sudden everyone's hugging and crying. You'd think we're running some sort of lonely-hearts club instead of a football camp. We've got to pull ourselves together."

"I take it you two worked things out," Red says with a smirk.

"We're solid, pal. Thanks!" I reply.

"Bringing me here to see my son is the greatest thing anyone has ever done for me," my father says to Red. "I'm eternally grateful to you."

"The pleasure's all mine," says Red. "You guys deserve it."

"So, why the waterworks with you and Belvedere?" I ask.

Red hesitates, letting out a big sigh. "This isn't easy for me to tell you, pal. In fact, I've been dreading it for a while, but it's time for me to move on."

"Whoa, wait a minute! Where's this coming from? Are you kidding me?" I ask in disbelief.

"It's no joke, Kyle. It's time for me to hang up my cleats. I've been at this for a long time and I can't stay here forever. I'm getting called upstairs."

"But we were just getting started. What about the camp?"

"You've got things under control. Heck, you transformed this entire place. It's already been cleared with the angels; they want you to take over."

"I'm not sure if I want to run this place, especially if you're leaving."

"You're going to do great things here. Belvedere wants to stay on board and Jessica will always be here for you."

"That's right, Kyle," says Jessica. "I'll be around to help you however I can."

"Hmm, I don't know. With all due respect, Jessica, you weren't able to do anything about the reincarnation issue and that's been a real problem for me."

"Kyle, this is your destiny," she sternly replies. "The specifics of your fate have recently been revealed to me."

"Well, by all means, can you please enlighten me?" I ask a bit sarcastically.

"From an early age," she says, "your love of football identified you as someone the angels had on their radar. Your potential, both as a player and beyond, held the promise of a tremendous career. However, when your heart condition cut your playing career short, you were never able to find another purpose in life that gave you that same passion. You were living an unfulfilled life, which was a bitter disappointment to you. At that point you were destined to end up in purgatory. Your accidental death set in motion the plan for you to meet Red, who has always been burdened during his time here by the guilt of not fulfilling the angels' request to restart the training camp. After you arrived and Red got a chance to know you, he would inevitably tell you about the camp in hopes of recruiting you to help bring it back. The experience would enable you to discover a new passion to give your spirit a meaningful purpose. By bringing the two of you together, you could help resolve each other's dilemmas and college football would be the ultimate benefactor."

"Well I'll be," says Red. "God sure does work in mysterious ways."

"Kyle, based on what you've already accomplished here in such a short time, you are clearly the right person for the job. If you stay, you can have a major impact on the future of the game. Now it's up to you to decide if you want to remain and continue your mission."

"If I decide not to, what happens then?"

"You are free to join Red in heaven and the camp will have to be shut down."

"If I leave, what happens to my father?"

"Eric, you broke a cardinal rule," says Jessica. "A human life is one of God's greatest gifts and taking yours put you in a perilous position. However, it has been decided that you have suffered enough hardship in your life. Therefore, you have been granted forgiveness and the right to enter heaven."

"Thank you, Jessica," my father says with a huge sigh of relief. "That's wonderful news!"

"What about the reincarnation problem, Jessica?" I ask. "I don't know if I want to stay here under those circumstances."

"It was anticipated this would remain a significant predicament for you and the matter has been deliberated at the highest levels. The future welfare of college football is of the utmost importance. Regarding the issue of CTE, it has been determined to be of such magnitude that the Archangel Raphael, the angel of physicians and healing, has been given a new mandate. He is to immediately guide researchers on earth to the discovery of the breakthroughs developed by Dr. Charcot and his team so that they can be put to use for the benefit of mankind without delay.

"This is a monumental occurrence for heaven to intercede in human affairs like this. Kyle, you are to be commended, as this is a direct result of your persistence in the matter that helped bring it into being.

"Moving forward, reincarnation will continue to be the method through which this camp will help evolve and advance the game for future generations. However, should other similarly groundbreaking innovations be developed that would have such a significant benefit to the game, they will be given full consideration to be immediately sent down to earth as well."

"What do you say, pal?" asks Red. "Sounds like a win-win to me."

"Hmm . . . all right, I'm in! Thanks for your help, Jessica."

"You're welcome, Kyle. Camp Grange is in good hands. Well, gentlemen," she says to Red and my father, "are you ready to go?"

My father hesitates for a moment and then comes over and puts his arm around my shoulders.

"If it's okay with everyone," he says, "I think I'd like to stay here and help my son."

"That's quite all right," says Jessica. "The gates of heaven will always be open for you. I know you'll make a great team here."

"Congratulations, fellas!" says Red, giving handshakes and hugs all around. "Well, Kyle, I guess this is it. I'm gonna miss you, pal. We had a heck of a ride!"

"We sure did," I say, struggling to fight off the sadness. "Dad, how about you and Belvedere grab some coffee and get acquainted—give Red and me a couple of minutes?"

"You bet, son," he says. "Belvedere, lead the way."

As they depart, I turn to my old friend, my mind racing to come up with ideas to keep him from leaving. "You really caught me off guard with your big announcement," I say.

"I know I should have given you more of a heads-up," Red says, "but I'm not very good at delivering bad news. I just figured ripping the bandage off was the best way to go."

"We've been so busy here," I say, "it never occurred to me that you might not always be along for the ride. What brought this on?"

"I've been in purgatory for a long time now. When things started to get rolling with the camp, I was hearing rumblings from upstairs that my time was up. They put me in this position as a kind of figurehead but I wasn't really giving anything back to the game. They wanted the camp back up and running and knew they needed a fresh spirit in here. You were the perfect one. I realize now that was their plan all along. You actually put me out of a job," he says jokingly.

"Well, hold on," I say. "I can change my mind. I'll tell them we're a package deal. You have to stay or I quit."

"No, I appreciate the gesture, but it's time to move on. I'm getting tired and feel myself slipping. I'm napping on the job just like they say Stagg used to do. Heck, I snapped us to a parking lot in Peoria when we should have been on campus in Champaign. That's never happened before. Besides, this *is* purgatory; no one's supposed to stay here forever. I'm sure they've got some sort of plan for me upstairs. The more I think about it, I'm kind of curious to see what heaven's all about, but I'll never forget our time here.

"I'm really proud of you, Kyle. You had a lot of tough breaks in your life, but you kept pushing to overcome those obstacles. You came here and have done a tremendous job. Your ideas and energy bringing this place back to life are beyond anything I could ever imagine. I know Walter Camp would be proud of how you've continued his mission. You've truly found a calling. My only regret for you is that you didn't have the playing career you hoped for on earth. Who knows, you might have made them completely forget about me down there."

"That would have been impossible," I reply. "Your heyday was nearly a hundred years ago and no matter how good anyone has been that followed, they've never forgotten you. You're a true legend and you're my best friend. It's painful to think how much I'll miss you."

"I feel the same way about you, pal," Red says. "I look forward to catching up when it's your time to join me up there. Listen, I've got to go now."

"Can't you stay a little while longer?" I ask. "I'd like to give you a going-away party. How about a parade?" I joke.

"I don't want a big fuss; I'm not much for good-byes," he says.

"At least let me round up the crew. I know they'd like to see you off."

"Thanks for the sentiment, but I'm going to slip out quietly. Please give them all my regards. Belvedere and I have already said our farewells. Be sure to pass along my best wishes to your dad."

"All right then, bring it in," I say with a final hug.

"Good-bye, pal," says the Ghost.

He takes a step back, giving a little wave and . . . Snap!

• • •

The office falls quiet with a saddening emptiness. Red's departure is a dispiriting loss. The Ghost led me on a journey that was the greatest experience of my entire existence.

I think back to some of the incredible adventures we had: the amazing rush from riding the buffalo at Colorado, the ponies at Oklahoma and the surreal flight on the wings of War Eagle. I'll never forget the crazy fun of wandering the Grove at Ole Miss and Red riding piggyback, howling the Illinois fight song in the middle of the crowd, unaware of the spectacle they were missing. I still get goose bumps recalling the trip back to 1924 watching the legend relive his greatest game.

I will always remember the countless discussions sharing our love of college football: reminiscing about the unique traditions, the bands, the fight songs, the tailgates and the bitter rivalries; never ceasing to be amazed at how student-athletes can give fans some of the most exciting moments and best memories of their lives.

I look back at my life on earth and wonder what could have been: living out my dreams of a successful playing career, meeting the right girl, getting married, raising a family and playing with my grandkids. What a different life that would have been, but I have no regrets.

I came to purgatory as a lost soul and discovered my destiny in a mission that fills my spirit with a passion that can burn till the end of time. Camp Grange consumes me with an unyielding drive to lead an enterprise capable of producing remarkable innovations for the benefit of the greatest sport on earth. There is nothing I'd rather be doing.

A quiet knocking at the door interrupts my daydream as Dad and Belvedere return.

"Sorry to intrude," my father says.

"Not at all, come on in," I say. "I'm glad you're back. Red had to leave rather suddenly but he sends his regards."

"I'm sorry I didn't get a chance to say good-bye," Dad says. "How are *you* doing?"

"I'm fine—doing great as a matter of fact," I reply, grateful to have my father and Belvedere here. "You know, I couldn't ask for two better partners to continue this journey with. We're gonna have a great time.

"Okay fellas, let's huddle up. We've got work to do!"

THE END

CPSIA information can be obtained
at www.ICGtesting.com
Printed in the USA
LVHW031103221221
706910LV00005B/150/J